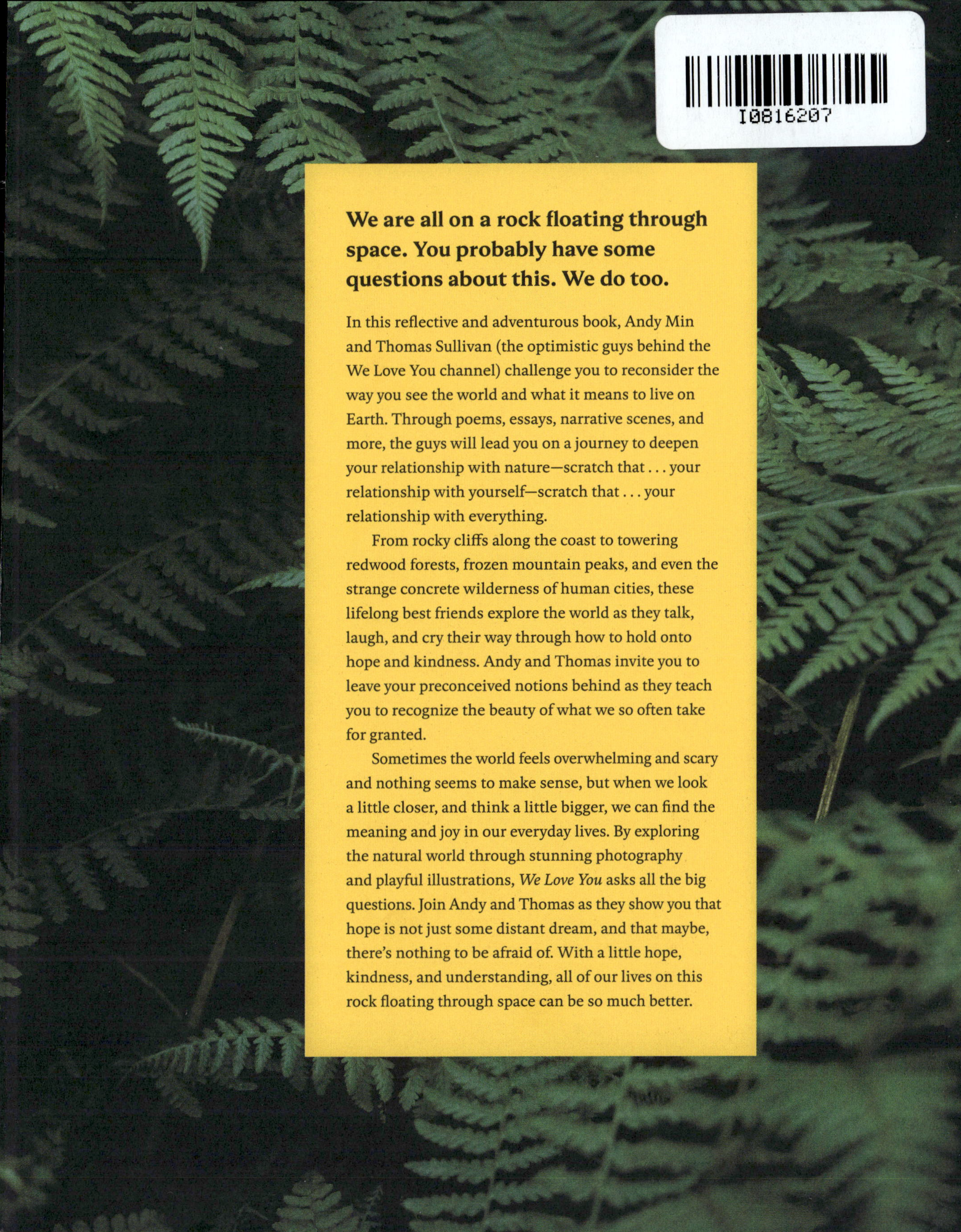

We are all on a rock floating through space. You probably have some questions about this. We do too.

In this reflective and adventurous book, Andy Min and Thomas Sullivan (the optimistic guys behind the We Love You channel) challenge you to reconsider the way you see the world and what it means to live on Earth. Through poems, essays, narrative scenes, and more, the guys will lead you on a journey to deepen your relationship with nature—scratch that . . . your relationship with yourself—scratch that . . . your relationship with everything.

From rocky cliffs along the coast to towering redwood forests, frozen mountain peaks, and even the strange concrete wilderness of human cities, these lifelong best friends explore the world as they talk, laugh, and cry their way through how to hold onto hope and kindness. Andy and Thomas invite you to leave your preconceived notions behind as they teach you to recognize the beauty of what we so often take for granted.

Sometimes the world feels overwhelming and scary and nothing seems to make sense, but when we look a little closer, and think a little bigger, we can find the meaning and joy in our everyday lives. By exploring the natural world through stunning photography and playful illustrations, *We Love You* asks all the big questions. Join Andy and Thomas as they show you that hope is not just some distant dream, and that maybe, there's nothing to be afraid of. With a little hope, kindness, and understanding, all of our lives on this rock floating through space can be so much better.

We Love You

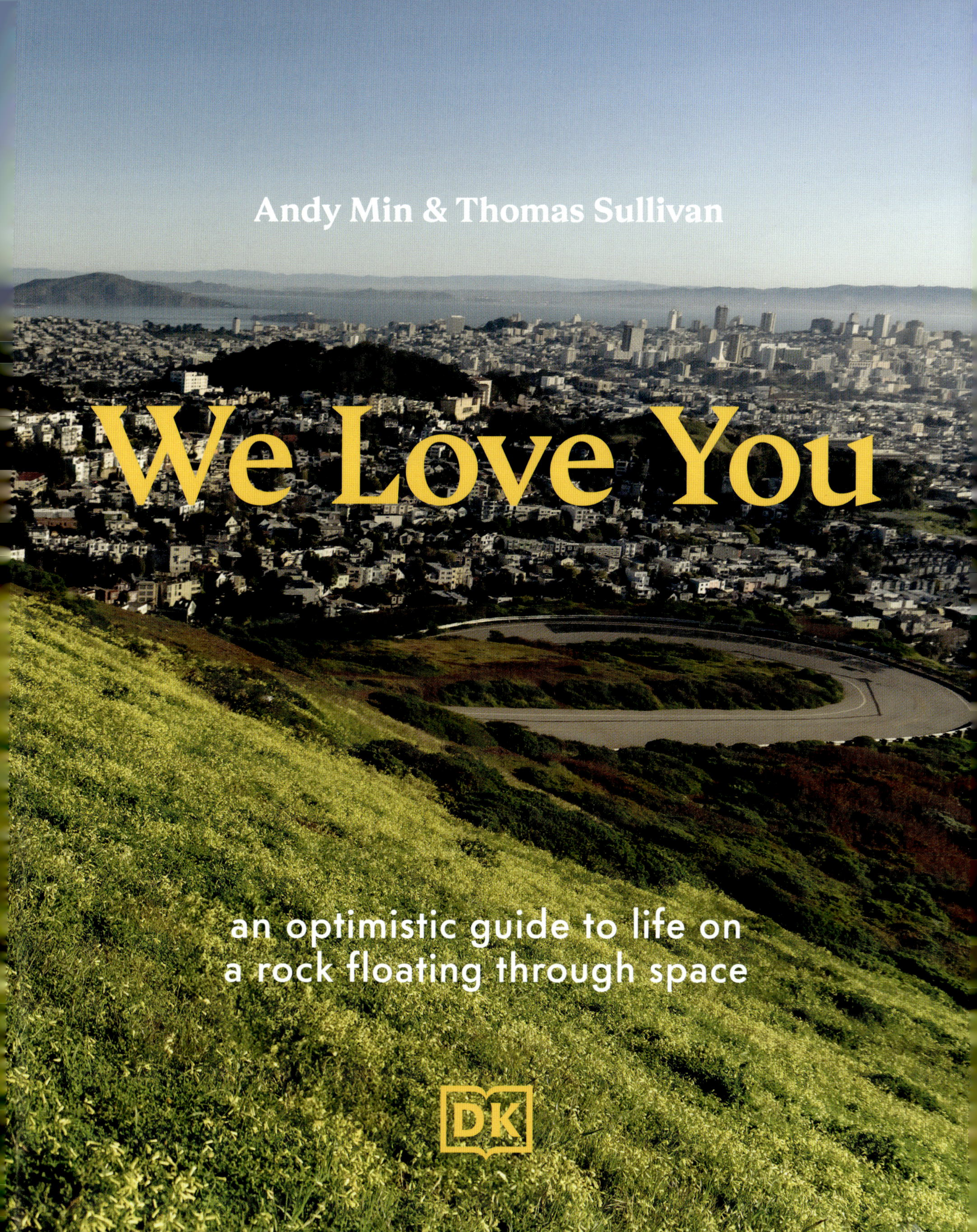
Andy Min & Thomas Sullivan
We Love You
an optimistic guide to life on
a rock floating through space
DK

Publisher Mike Sanders
Executive Editor Alexander Rigby
Editorial Director Ann Barton
Art & Design Director William Thomas
Designer Joanna Price
Primary Photographer Mark McInnis
Primary Illustrator Dávid Pogran
Editorial Assistant Resham Anand
Copy Editors Tiffany Taing, Michael Trudeau
Proofreaders Jaye Whitney Debber, Mira S. Park

First American Edition, 2025
Published in the United States by DK Publishing
1745 Broadway, 20th Floor, New York, NY 10019

The authorized representative in the EEA is Dorling Kindersley Verlag GmbH. Arnulfstr. 124, 80636 Munich, Germany

25 26 27 28 29 10 9 8 7 6 5 4 3 2 1
001-345714-OCT2025

Library of Congress Number: 2025936560
ISBN 978-0-5939-6413-2

DK books are available at special discounts when purchased in bulk for sales promotions, premiums, fundraising, or educational use. For details, contact SpecialSales@dk.com

Printed and bound in Italy by L.E.G.O. S.p.A.

www.dk.com

This book was made with Forest Stewardship Council™ certified paper – one small step in DK's commitment to a sustainable future.
Learn more at **www.dk.com/uk/information/sustainability**

For our mothers,
fathers, and brothers.

Thanks for teaching us
what love means.

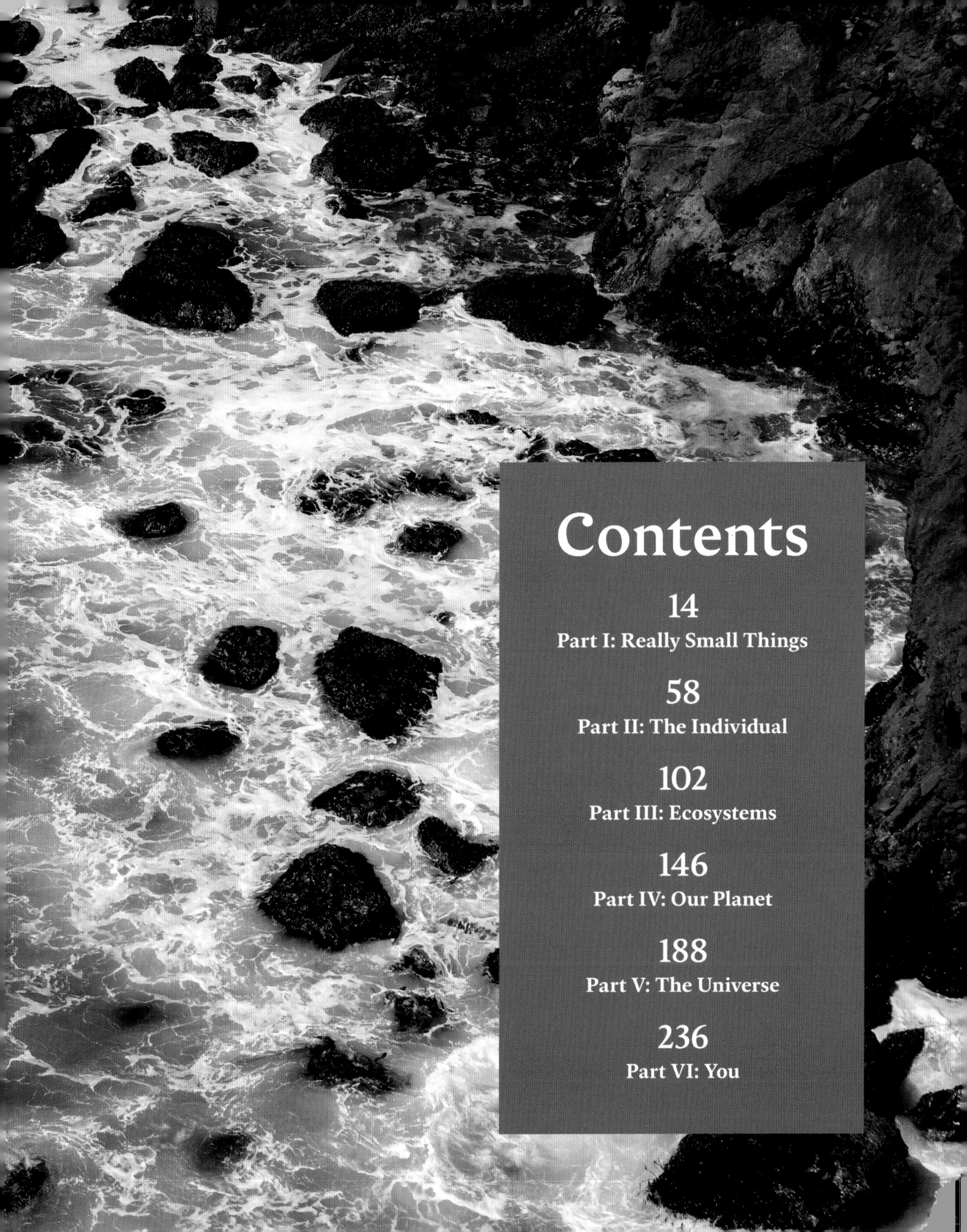

Contents

Introduction

Hey, man!

You might not always like to think about it, but right now you are on a rock floating through the infinite nothingness of space. Your entire world—from the smallest ant to the tallest redwood, from the salamander's den to the highest mountain peak, from your dearest family and friends to the most distant stranger, and from your greatest fears to your favorite sandwich—exists on a tiny speck of dust drifting aimlessly through the void. And you are here too.

We all are.

We have a lot of questions about this, just like you probably do. How? Why? Are we going to be OK? We don't claim to have all the answers, but by looking a little closer and thinking a little bigger, we might be able to find a way through together.

We're Thomas and Andy. You might know us from the videos we post online under the name We Love You. We've connected with our audience by asking each other the big questions—just like we've been doing since we became best friends back in the sixth grade—and turning those conversations into short films. We frame our work through a radically optimistic lens, and we are so grateful that our videos have helped people see the beauty and silver linings in the world. But the truth is, we haven't always seen the world this way. It's only through our own struggles with the big questions that we've learned to see the good.

Life is not always easy. Forests can be dark, cities can be loud, and people can be . . . well, you know how people can be. Often the world feels too big to make sense of, too difficult to try to change for the better. All the while, the entire world is just one tiny part of our big, scary universe. On the grand scale of life, we are all very, very small, and our one and only lives are very, very short. We know this is a lot to make sense of, but don't ignore these truths just because they scare you. This is the situation we're all in.

Our goal is not to show you that everything is perfect and lovely exactly as it is. There is a lot of work to do. There will always be things that are hard to accept. Yet even in a scary world, you can still find kindness. We want you to realize that even when you feel completely hopeless, there is still hope.

Through the poems, essays, scenes, and everything else across these pages, we'll try to help you find that hope. A lot of it is stuff you might already know. We haven't invented new formulas for happiness or done groundbreaking research. We've just lived our lives, trying our best to see the world as it really is, all while striving not to take anything for granted. We are just two people spinning on the same speck of dust that you are, looking out at the absurd, beautiful world we've all been born into, trying to notice the good we see and put it into words. We're all on this Earth together. So, we must find a way toward love, kindness, and hope as we all live our lives on this rock floating through space.

We hope you like it.

We love you.

Take Nothing for Granted

Try looking at the world in front of you with totally open eyes. What would you think if the scene in front of you as you read this was the first thing, the first moment, you had ever experienced? What sort of questions would you have? What would you be fascinated by?

What about this moment would amaze you if you were in a position to take absolutely nothing for granted? The answer, of course, is that you would be amazed by just about everything.

Looking out at the world, you might wonder what that bright thing in the sky is, the one that hurts your eyes if you look at it. You might wonder what the deal is with all this green. If this was the first moment you ever experienced, you might question what this strange new consciousness means in the first place.

This book follows this very idea: To understand the world, we must learn to take absolutely nothing for granted. If we want to truly experience the world, we have to put aside the numbness and habituation we've built up through our lives to let in the unbelievable wonder that constantly surrounds us. We have to live as if this is our first time seeing the world and that every thing matters, because this *is* our first time seeing the world, and maybe, every thing *does* matter.

There are things we might be more comfortable forgetting rather than facing head-on—mortality, the never-ending march of time, the dark sides of human nature, and the mysteries of what existence even is. There are answers we will never have and we are only here for so long. So, why should you spend your time asking these uncomfortable questions?

It would be easier to concentrate just on the ordinary things, on the day-to-day triumphs and struggles of a standard, sensible human life. But the thing is, that isn't the world we actually live in.

From the smallest insect to the largest galaxy, from the existence of dark matter to our own human existence, nothing is simple and nothing is ordinary. Paying close attention to the extraordinary nature of our lives can be scary, but it is also how we can start to see just how beautiful everything really is. It is up to each and every one of us to see the wonder of it all and, maybe, to find the meaning within all the stunning shapes, colors, and sounds. Because, we promise you, everything, no matter how big or small, has meaning. If you look closely, you might find that it all means something to you too.

In the face of all these "whys,"
life just is.

Part I

REALLY SMALL THINGS

There Is Good News

What if
you had never
seen anything?

What if
you had never
felt a cool breeze
on your cheek?

What if
you had never
heard the waves crashing,
your mother's voice,
the birds calling
in the morning?

What if
you had never
existed at all?

Never
thought anything,
known anything,
been anything?

It's hard to imagine.
Timeless,
spaceless,
invisible,
nothing at all.

But what would you think
if you were born into existence
this very moment?
Staring in awe at
the world in front of you,
the sun on your skin,
and other things just like you,
all around.

What would you do
if you had only this
one window
into being?

To see with open eyes,
to feel without knowing,
to love without reason.

What would you do
if this was the only
life you had?

There is good news.

Mud

Let's start with something small and something simple: mud.

It's the grimy stuff along the edges of the sidewalk after it rains. It's in your potted plants after you water them. It gets stuck to your shoes on a trail and clings to them for days after the storm you hiked through has come and gone. You see it glistening along the side of the road and don't give it a second thought. As a kid, you probably came home covered in it more than once, only to be sent quickly to the bathroom to scrub yourself clean, with muddy footprints following in your wake. It's as simple as it gets.

As hard as the world is to understand, as difficult as life gets, as painful as it can be to carry around all our big, unanswered questions, you can always trust that mud is never far away. Isn't that a nice thing?

We can't escape the fact that this planet is made of mud. At our highest highs and at our lowest lows, our old friend mud is still with us. We grow our food in it, we stomp in it, and eons ago, we may have come from it. One day, we will all gently return to it.

You may remember a moment in your life when, for one reason or another, everything felt wrong. Heartbroken, grief-stricken, or lost, you walked home, to school, or around the block just to get outside, and like clockwork, the sky cracked open and down came the rain. Suddenly, the solid ground underneath your feet became soft, dark, and slick, and all around you was a world of mud. Maybe you slipped in it, or maybe you just smelled the rich earth breathing the water in, as if taunting you.

But the thing is, mud doesn't know how to taunt. And we bet if it did, it wouldn't want to. During those sad moments—when your heart aches and your nights feel aimless—aren't you glad that out there in the world, rain is still turning dirt into mud as usual?

Now, as the rain pours down around you and everything turns to mud, don't imagine the world is crying with you or that the soil is laughing at your pain. Instead, imagine the light-brown dirt changing into dark-brown mud, as the water mixes with the earth to become something new. Of course, this takes no imagination at all, because it is exactly what is happening. The cool water and the living earth combine. Like the transformation of the hero in a great story, like the first stars starting to burn, like your very life beginning not so long ago, something becomes something else. Can't you see how wonderful this truly is?

If it helps, picture the rain-dimpled mud spreading out all around you and curving upward into a wide, gentle smile. And try, if you can, to imagine yourself smiling too. Then, let the rain fall, and stomp through the mud, toward home.

You are mud.

There is more going on in a single patch of mud than you could ever fathom . . .

The Invisible World

Let's get up close to some mud and see what it's made of. Close up, the simple brown sludge we carefully step over in our day-to-day actually becomes pretty interesting. What seems like homogeneous muck suddenly takes a new shape. You may notice sticks, crushed leaves, acorns, or the decaying exoskeletons of ants and flies. If you're lucky, a bold little worm may appear, wiggling its way along the surface. Looking closer, you might see that no two spots of mud are exactly alike—some are a little lighter or darker than others, and some have different consistencies altogether. You may notice that the dark spots are rich with decaying plant matter, with bits of narrow roots and leaves sticking out, while the light spots are more fluid and claylike, with tiny silt grains rolling between your fingers as you pinch the mud between them. Even in a random patch of muddy ground, there really is a lot to see.

But wait, we've barely scratched the surface!

If we were to take a glob of mud and put it under a microscope to magnify it even more, we'd see an entire world of life teeming and wriggling around in minuscule forms. There are tiny insects, amoebas, and nematodes by the thousands darting around every inch of the wet soil beneath our feet. There is more going on in a single patch of mud than you could ever fathom, and it's all happening on a scale so small it's practically invisible to us.

It's hard to believe, and even easier to forget, that entire lives—though incredibly simple and small—are playing out many times over in every handful of mud. What kind of life does a nematode live, wriggling away in the muddy puddle next to a pond? As small as they are, we like to think that maybe, somehow, they are happy.

But what if we go closer?

What if we zoom in past the nematodes, past the tiny worms and mosquito larvae? What if we try to find something that even nematodes would call tiny? Going more microscopic, a more intricate ecosystem comes into view. Single-cellular life appears by the millions and billions. Protists and algae hunt and photosynthesize, while bacteria—a thousand times smaller than nematodes—crawl around everywhere you can see. A thousand times smaller still, viruses wage an invisible war, infecting and populating the microscopic world. In a single teaspoon of mud, there are more bacteria than there are people on Earth. But this doesn't apply just to mud—everywhere we look, there is a microscopic universe of life. Rivers and lakes burst with life in every drop of water, and each leaf on the trees in

your neighborhood hosts critters of every shape and size. Your kitchen counter, the desk in front of you, the page or device you're reading from, and even the hand that's holding this book are all teeming with life of every kind. And all of it is eating and procreating and fighting for existence all at once—just like us.

You're probably thinking, *"OK, yeah . . . I get that life is everywhere. I kind of already knew that, though. I guess it is a little gross, but why does it matter?"*

It matters because we are life. When you look at things closely, you start to see that even the smallest living things, the most common life-forms in the known universe, are actually pretty exciting. Looking down at a creature that's invisible to the naked eye with a microscope reveals its complex shapes and the way it moves, as you watch in awe. You might even be amazed. This thing is here. It's a real part of the world, the same world you're a part of, and it's unbelievably, defiantly alive.

When we look at these tiny, individual specimens, something becomes clear: Even this smallest unit of life is startling and beautiful. Every component of life is worthy of being noticed, of capturing your wonder and, maybe in some microscopic way, your love. If you can find a tiny sliver of care or beauty in your heart for the tiny lives that surround us, the world becomes a bit more full and more spectacular. If you hold on to that sliver of care in your mind, and scale it up a million times in size, intensity, and complexity, maybe then you'll understand just how big we all really are.

Every component of life is worthy of being noticed . . .

Atoms and Friends

We are sitting on a rock outcropping on a hiking trail halfway up the Yosemite Valley. I take a long swig from my water bottle and look at the view below us. Sheer granite rock walls surround the tree-filled valley on every side. It is autumn, and clusters of aspens are starting to turn yellow, like gems in a sea of evergreen. The view before us feels enormous and all-encompassing, but I notice Andy is looking at something tiny right in front of him, very intently.

"What's this made of?" Andy asks as he hefts up a round, speckled rock about the size of a golf ball to get a good look at it. He tosses the rock in my direction, and I catch it.

"What do you mean? It's just a rock," I say. I throw the rock back to Andy and try to refocus on the view.

"No, I know that. But what is it *made of*?" Andy asks, tossing the stone to me yet again.

I take a closer look at the round granite rock. For a second, the light catches a crystal on the surface, illuminating it in silvery specks.

"Well, it's made of different rocks and minerals and stuff. Right?" I say, half sure, and toss him the rock back.

"Right." Andy looks closer at the black specks of mica. "But what is *that* made of?"

"Dude . . . " I say.

"I'm just asking!" He shrugs.

"OK, well, a lot of rocks are made of silica molecules." I think back to high school geology as I catch the stone he tosses to me once more, with both hands. I know as soon as I say it that this answer isn't enough to satisfy either of us.

Andy takes a breath in and winces. "But what is that made—"

I cut him off. "I think it's made of silicon and oxygen. Right?" Looking at the rock in my hand, I see that there really isn't any easy answer to what I'm holding.

"Right. Oxygen. The atom. The fundamental unit of matter." Andy nods, for a moment letting the mystery hang in the air. The questions ask themselves: What is an atom? What are *they* made of? We both want to know.

"Yep," I say, and look out at Half Dome, which suddenly doesn't seem so big.

Andy looks around for a moment. He places his hands in front of him like he's holding an invisible beach ball, then sighs. "So, oxygen has . . . " he begins.

"Eight protons, eight neutrons, eight electrons," I say, knowing that my answer only raises more questions. I toss him the rock, and he catches it without hardly looking.

"Right." He looks deeply at the rock, as if he can see the endless particles in it vibrating. "So those are . . ."

"Those are the smallest things. Protons are positive; electrons are negative. They balance each other out. They make up everything. Periodic table, all that jazz." I try to give this answer an air of finality, but neither of us are quite convinced.

"Right. Cool." Andy pauses again, considering what to say next. "But what about quarks? Aren't those smaller?"

"Oh, yeah, quarks technically make up everything. *They're* the fundamental constituents of all matter . . ." I trail off, realizing something. "Wait. You knew about quarks this whole time? Why are you asking me, then?"

"I just wanted to talk about how crazy it is!" Andy throws the rock in an overhand lob. It overshoots and hits the tree behind me. "Like all of this! That rock, the mountains, the air, me and you—the whole world is made of the same magical stuff!"

"I guess it is pretty crazy." I look around. The golf-ball-size rock on the ground by the foot of the tree. The valley below us full of life. The river running through it. The clear air surrounding us. I can almost see the particles it's all made of: these totally different things that, somehow, are built with the same tiny stuff. It seems so absurd, that we go our whole lives without ever really acknowledging it.

"Hey, man?" Andy asks, staring out at the valley.

"Yeah?" I respond, looking at Half Dome again in awe.

"I think I'm thinking about it too much," he says.

"Yeah, me too. *Big* time," I say.

When we start to realize that every element in the world, including ourselves, is made up of tiny, vibrating mysteries, it changes our perspective. Everything feels a little more amazing and makes us feel closer to the wonderful mystery at the root of it all. Whatever our strange world is made of, we are made from it too.

Whatever our strange world is made of, we are made from it too.

The Building Blocks of Everything

Everything is made of atoms. Every single thing you can imagine is built of tiny particles clumped together in different ways, with slightly different properties. An atom itself is made up of mostly empty space with a dense proton-neutron core surrounded by electron orbitals (where the electrons *might* be).

In the last hundred and fifty years, we've learned a lot about the atom, but there is still so much we don't understand. At the smallest level, the fundamental mysteries of physics and reality come into full display: Where did all this stuff come from? How does it work? And the biggest question of all: Why? These existential questions are woven into every aspect of life: the walls, the sidewalk, the tree outside, and even your own hands. The most ordinary things are made up of these tiny particles. *All of it* is atoms.

Really ponder this for a moment. You are atoms! The birds are atoms! The toaster is atoms! Your phone is atoms! The air you are breathing is atoms! Don't brush it off as one of those things you *know* but don't really think about. Because when you start to focus on this reality, it's actually kind of crazy. Your whole world is made of unimaginably small particles with strange behaviors, mind-bending rules, and endless mysteries. If you're *really* thinking about it, the very thought alone can send your mind spinning. Where did all these atoms come from? What is it all for? Where do I fit in to all this? How do we see the world differently, with the understanding that a solid brick wall is made mostly of empty space? How are we supposed to make peace with the knowledge that everything we see and touch is made of unimaginably small units of matter that we don't fully understand? How do we make peace with the fact that we are made of this stuff too?

These are all good questions to ask, because so much of our world feels separate from these big ideas. Too often we live on autopilot. Sure, we have desires and fears, and we think about where we are going to be a week into the future, but we're not usually paying attention to the deepest truth of our situation.

Sometimes we feel bored and tune out. We feel distant from our lives and disinterested in the world. We are pulled from day to day by wants and worries, but somehow none of it feels like enough. We know there are big questions out there being asked by physicists and philosophers, but none of it feels quite real—these big mysteries are somewhere else and certainly not right in front of us. But that's because too often we don't look around and *really* see

the world. Instead we see what is most efficient and simple. We are accustomed to everything we are and everything we have. We take reality for granted. We forget about the unbelievable wonder surrounding us on all sides. We forget how we are made of little particles that were once sent flying out from the stars. We forget that the world *is* atoms.

Try taking a moment to observe whatever it is you might be looking at, and say to yourself, "This is atoms." And try your best to see them. *Know* they are there.

This exercise might feel a little weird to do, but it's supposed to. Looking closely at your ordinary life and recognizing that the inexplicable secrets of the universe are right in front of you every second is a little uncomfortable. Suddenly, a chair isn't just a chair, something to look at and use but not pay much attention to. A chair is a collection of specific atoms accumulated in the wood of a tree and harvested by human hands (also atoms), shaped to serve the abstract concept of a chair. The greatest unknowns of our existence are threaded through every square inch of it.

Don't forget these facts. When we keep the uncomfortable truth at the forefront of our minds instead of pushing it away, a scary revelation quickly becomes something more. Instead of seeing the world as the plain and boring background you usually tune out, every little thing becomes amazing. Every corner of your life—the entire world you live in—bursts with wonder, allowing you to more easily see the beauty right in front of you. A chair is not just a chair. A tree is not just a tree. A person is not just a person. Each and every thing is worth noticing. This isn't some fantastical way of looking at things. This is how it has always been, even though you might be seeing it only now. This is how the world actually is. This is your life.

This is how we can realize that *absolutely nothing is ordinary.*

. . . nothing is ordinary.

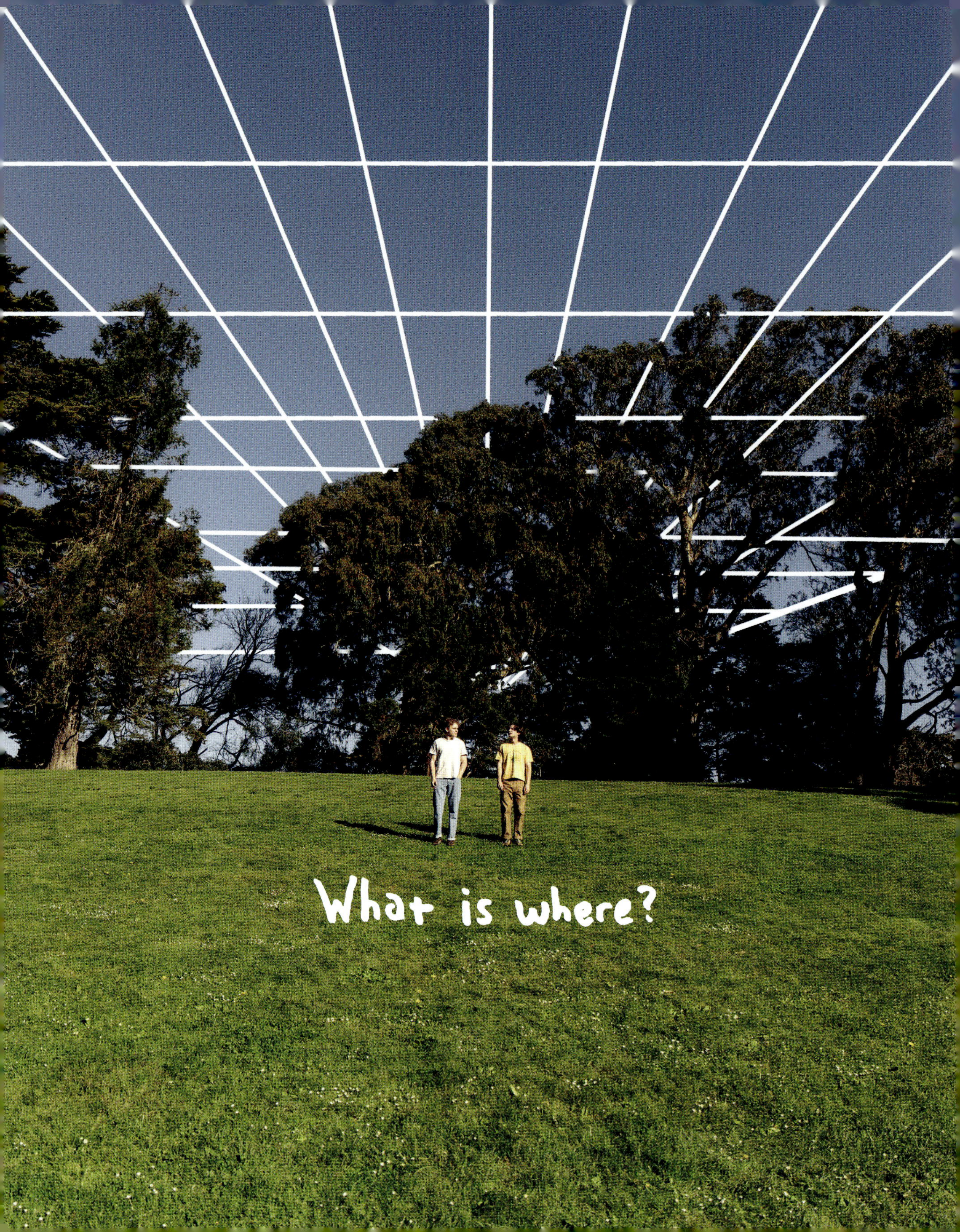
What is where?

Where Are You Right Now?

Look around the space you're currently inhabiting. Maybe there are walls and a chair, or maybe you're sitting outside, with a river rushing by from left to right. You could be in a crowded coffee shop, where strangers are laughing and talking all around you. You could be anywhere.

As you look around, what do you notice? You might notice a little cobweb in the corner of your room by the ceiling, fluttering gently from an imperceptible draft. You might study how the river water moves through space from there to here. You might watch as people move around the coffee shop in winding, determined arcs to get from one place to another.

These are all normal, everyday scenarios, the kinds of things you often pay no mind to. Wind flutters, water flows, and people go about their business. What we're going to say next might sound a bit silly at first, but please, stick with us here. Take another look around, and *for one moment, try not to take it for granted that you live in three-dimensional space.*

Entertain the notion that just because left, right, up, down, forward, and backward are the directions you know and have moved through your whole life, it doesn't necessarily mean that it's the only way a world could be. What if there were another direction to move in? Why are there three dimensions of space instead of two or one? You might find yourself wondering why there is any space at all. We must ask ourselves not just *where are we?*, but *what is where?*

Really try to question this. If it helps, move your hand around a little bit (in circles or back and forth, whichever you prefer). Watch as your hand moves farther from your face, seemingly shrinking in size and arriving somewhere two feet or so away. What is happening there? Yes, your hand is moving from one place to another, crossing a distance to get there—but *what really is a place? What really is a distance?* A place is a point in space, and a distance is the difference between two points. But let's keep going—what is space? What is this stuff we move through? Take a moment, take a breath, and really look around and see it.

Of course, there are scientific definitions and explanations that give us some answers, but they aren't what we're seeking here. We want to go deeper. Just because we have words to describe something doesn't make it any less amazing. What does space mean to you? If you can, see beyond this spatial reality you're accustomed to, and you'll start to see what's really in front of you, if only for a moment.

The restless cobweb in the corner of your room isn't just some mess to be cleaned up; it's a cozy nest where a creature found shelter amid the vast cosmic expanse. The river rushing through the valley isn't only a passing sight; it is a vector of motion churning through the mystery of space-time. The people in the coffee shop or at the park walking from one point to another are accomplishing no small feat, reaching destinations with purpose.

If we keep our eyes forward, we can navigate through the confounding journey of life—the one we have no choice but to face every moment that passes. Our feet move up and down, our lungs breathe in and out, and our hands swing at our sides, sometimes miles and miles from home.

It can feel daunting—the never-ending motion from here to there, the mystery of how to get anywhere, the mystery of being anywhere at all. But when we reach our destinations, determined and glad, we know we are exactly where we're supposed to be.

From Here to There

Sometimes, I feel like I will never be happy again,
and then I go on a bike ride.
The world rushes into motion around me on every side.
Yes, I am still breathing.
Yes, I can move with my own legs
through these three dimensions of space.

Sometimes, it feels like no one in the world knows me,
and then I turn left to roll down the hill.
The wind in my face knows me,
and the trees turning pink in the sunset
know something about me too:
that I am made of the same stuff they are,
that I don't need to be anything besides what I am.

Sometimes, I hate that there are
things I will never understand.
Why is the world shaped like it is?
How do you get from here to there?

But now, I am riding my bike,
and I am going somewhere,
so the questions don't seem so big.
Everything makes as much sense as it has to
for the world—and these wheels—to keep spinning,
even if it makes no sense at all.

Somehow, that feels like an answer.
Somehow, almost all at once,
I am happy.

One Second

As you are reading this, something is happening. Look around you. Even if nothing seems to be moving, something is rushing by every second: *time*. While your eyes move across this page and your lungs breathe air into your body, the seconds tick by one by one, moving you and the whole world into the future. Time is one of those things that is too far-reaching and fundamental to wrap our heads around. So, maybe to avoid getting too mind-bending too fast, we have to set aside the cosmic mystery of time as a whole, and zoom all the way in, to focus on just one second.

Picture a patch of empty sky. It hangs inert and empty. But count in your head for just one second, and everything changes. A bolt of lightning crashes through the air, fracturing into millions of snaking lines. A crack of thunder thrums across the previously silent sky. By the time you get to "two Mississippi," the world is a different place. As you watch, your life changes by the second too. Like the flash of lightning, an idea is had, a memory is formed, or a decision is made, fractalizing into spindling webs of light, changing the course of all that is still to come. It doesn't stop there. In an instant, lives are born brightly into existence, and just as swiftly, lives dissipate into complete absence. In a single second, there is history, just as there is the loudness of a million leaves falling swiftly onto the soft forest floor.

Take a moment to imagine a garden earthworm with a lifespan of three years wriggling through a warm bed of compost. How long does a second feel to this worm? A Greenland shark can live for up to four hundred years, continuously swimming through the cold depths of Arctic waters, searching for its next measly meal of krill. How long does that same second feel to the shark? Is it faster or slower than it is for the worm?

Based on our human perception of time, where time speeds up exponentially as we age, we might assume that a second would go by faster for the shark. But maybe the Greenland shark, swimming in the glacial waters, unencumbered by the worries of humans, understands each second better because it has lived through so many more than the worm has, so many more than we have too. Maybe the shark is not counting down to its inevitable demise; maybe instead it's adding that one second to its continued collection of time, knowledge, life, and shark enlightenment that we humans may never understand. If you had the lifespan of an earthworm, would you use your seconds, minutes, days, and weeks any differently? What if you had the lifespan of a Greenland shark? What might happen across all these new seconds being laid out in front of you?

We all think we know what a second feels like. If I were to ask you to count to "ten Mississippi," your timing would probably be just about right. But a second spent stuck in traffic or scrolling on your phone vanishes entirely and without warning, like it never belonged to you at all. All these seconds blur as they leave us, as the present second facing us becomes something different.

When you focus intently on the steady *click-clack* of the seconds ticking by, tuning in to every moment slipping away, time can be a scary thing. The future

fades into the present and the present fades into the past far too quickly for anyone to hold on to. At one moment or another in our lives, we might wish to pause where we are and stretch that single moment across eternity—to linger in the feeling of the warm embrace of home or to sit in the beauty of the last hues of a sunset for as long as we can. Time moves, indifferent to our longing, no matter where we are. Each second soon becomes history, each hour slipping away from our fingertips like water. We wish we didn't have to face the inevitability that this moment, this second, month, and year, all of it will end. The future, with all its great unknowns, looms large over us, casting a very long shadow.

Here's the thing: The future doesn't really exist. Neither does the past. They exist only in our minds. All there ever really is is one long string of *right nows*. Our entire lives are made up of seconds. If you can find peace and joy in the one second in front of you, the dark cloud of time's passage starts to clear. Isn't it comforting to know that no matter what may come, no matter how big or overwhelming our future may feel, when it actually gets here, it can only come at us one second at a time?

. . . we know we're here, right now. And right now is pretty cool.

What Is Time?

The blue ocean water crashes into the shoreline. We stand where the water meets the sand, letting the waves pass close by our feet. The water ebbs and flows, sinking our shoes deeper into the sand wave by wave.

"Hey, man? I'm worried," I say as the water retreats.

"Oh . . . thinking about time again? What's up?" Thomas replies.

I nod. The sun is high in the sky, making the heavens look as blue as the sea. I try to figure out how to put my thoughts into words.

"So, if time is like a train, and that train keeps on going in one direction—or, um—that isn't what I really mean. Time isn't just tracks that we follow; it's bigger than that. If time is like a boat sailing on the open ocean, and it's always moving in the same way the wind blows, and there's no way to stop the boat or get off it, it's like it's impossible to ever actually *be anywhere*. Or in any moment. It's all so fleeting."

The waves crash raucously, pelting our pants with an abrasive mix of icy seawater and suspended sand.

"I know what you mean," Thomas says. A flock of seagulls crosses the afternoon sky, calling out in their usual spectral squawks. Thomas watches them fly by. "But I guess it depends on how you think about it."

"How so?" I ask.

"Like, maybe time isn't as simple as a boat moving through water or a train running along tracks. Maybe that's just how it feels to us."

"Almost like we're the boat, and time is what? The ocean of every single moment, past and future?"

Thomas nods, but I can tell he isn't convinced. I rub my temple and try to reconcile just how difficult it is to picture time as an abstract concept.

"But wouldn't that mean we have other directions to go? Wouldn't that mean that even though we've moved away from one moment, somehow the past still exists somewhere?" The questions spill out of me.

"Yeah, maybe . . . maybe not . . . I don't know, man," Thomas replies, not sure how else to answer me.

We both take in deep breaths and linger in our confusion. Another wave crashes and washes over our shoes, which are quickly becoming wet.

"Maybe we're not like a boat or a train, or even moving at all," Thomas says, trying to frame his response in a different way. "Maybe that's just what it feels like for some reason. It could be more that we're part of something like the ocean; maybe we're the water."

The sea spreads out all the way to the horizon. It ripples and reflects the sun, moving and rising with the winds and tides. I don't know if this is the right answer either, but something feels right about it.

"Whatever it is, we know we're here, right now. And right now is pretty cool," Thomas says.

I nod and chuckle. "Bah! What even is time, anyway?"

Thomas gives me a sly look and glances down at his phone and replies. "Ehh, I'd say it's about 1:30."

It's not exactly the answer I want, but it'll have to do.

Perception

The world is not as you see it. This might be a little troubling to think about at first, but don't worry—it's going to be OK. We've encouraged you to zoom in pretty closely to the tiny elements that make up our world, and hopefully you've started seeing that there's so much more around you than meets the eye. When you try to experience everything around you without taking it for granted, you recognize how amazing life is. But now, let's take another step closer. Instead of looking at the smallest things, maybe we should be looking at the act of looking itself.

Everything we're able to see and experience in our world, no matter how mundane, can reach us only through our windows of perception. Our entire lives are experienced through the power of our five senses, the vehicles through which we come to explore the world: hearing, sight, smell, taste, and touch. Our senses are incredibly capable tools that allow our bodies and minds to operate and interact with our environment, but it's important to remember: They are not the world itself.

Imagine a banana slug. It has spent its whole life in the shade, on the side of a hill amid a cluster of trees not too far from a babbling stream. It looks out through its strange almost-eyes, which exist at the ends of its optical tentacles. Able to see only a few feet in front of itself and sensing the difference between shade and light, the banana slug feels the world beneath it through the nerves of its slimy body. It makes its way over decomposing stumps in the forest, leaving a trail of slime over soft wood and pine needles, which rub up against its mucus-coated underside as it moves. Envision what the world must appear like to this slug. Does the slug see the world as it really is? Or is there a chance that the slug's limited senses, which developed to perceive only what is most crucial for survival, do not give it a complete picture of the infinitely intricate world we live in? Chances are pretty good that's the case. And if that's true for the slug, on some level, the same has to be true for us.

As intelligent and on top of things as we may feel we are as a species, each of us has a pretty limited view of the world. As closely as we magnify the small aspects or as big of a picture as we want to see, we can interpret the elements only through our limited array of biological senses.

When we think more deliberately about how our senses work, it may be a bit uncomfortable to focus more acutely on how we experience reality. It may seem reductive and mechanical. Our entire world, everything we know about life—the entire universe even—has come to us through five clusters of sensory neurons, two of which are basically dedicated to whether or not we want to eat something. To us, our day-to-day lives feel clear and complete, not a

What do
you see?

patchwork recorded and reported by wet nodes in our noses, hairs in our ears, or gelatinous film in the backs of our eyes. It's our life. It is the world as we know it. Breaking this world down into rudimentary inputs can be scary. It can make us feel small. Instead of experiencing the sensible, busy human lives we're used to, suddenly we may feel like animals, like slugs crawling along the bottom of a log with no idea of the world they live in. But when we take the time to sit with our limited perceptions of the world, we start to realize there isn't anything to be afraid of.

We see the setting sun with our eyes. We hear the river roaring with our ears. We smell the morning dew with our noses. We taste the fresh bread with our mouths. We feel the warmth of our friend's hand with our skin. No, after all, we are not slugs. We are humans, and these are the ways a human comes to know the world. What else could we want?

Yes, there is probably more to the world than what we are able to experience with our limited palette of senses. What you're able to witness is but a small window into what all there may be, a thought that can be a bit unnerving. You may ask yourself: What are we missing? What is the truth? What is the world, really? These are not questions with concrete answers, but that doesn't mean you shouldn't ask them. Sometimes, it is when there are the fewest answers that we can learn the most.

If you get close enough to the world, you start to see your own reflection, and this is exactly how it should be, because maybe your reflection is worth looking at. You are the only one in our universe who can see it through your eyes, and maybe that is all you need.

This isn't to say that reality can be anything you want it to be, or that you can decide your own answers for every question. We are saying that the world is made of questions, that *you* are part of this world, and that you are a question too.

To remember that we can't see everything, and to learn to love each thing we can see—perhaps *that* is the way to see the world as it really is.

Bugs and Creepy-Crawlies

What if we told you that under a decaying log in the wet redwood forests of the Santa Cruz Mountains there lies an entire universe with its own inhabitants, rules, and mysteries? Lift up said log: roly-polies in their knight's armor parade around, some rolling up into their tiny shells to protect themselves from the mammalian beast staring directly at them. There are leaf-cutter ants marching in line, holding leaves quadruple the size of their bodies. Do they know there is an entire planet spinning beneath their very legs? Can we understand the lives they lead? Do they even think about their lives as their own? Ants are a hive mind, caring only about the will of the colony. To them, an individual life is a worthy sacrifice for the greater good of the colony. Would said ant, brainwashed by the authoritarian nature of its society, rebel if it understood the advances in democracy and individuality that its fellow earthlings have made in human society? Or would it still care only for the greater good of its colony? Does an ant know that its entire life will occur in the span of just three to four square miles? With so many little lives wriggling away all around the world, we can't help but imagine that they know something we don't. We can't help but wonder: Are they happy?

A caterpillar writhes its way out of the log and climbs up a nearby tree, coming to rest on a cozy hammock-shaped leaf. It eats and eats, spindling itself a waxy cocoon, disintegrating into a gooey, soupy womb, only to eventually break free from its self-imposed chrysalis as a butterfly. Was that its goal? Does it feel a fleeting moment of contentment as it takes flight for the first time, only to recognize that its days are now more numbered than ever? Can a butterfly have a midlife crisis? Our guess is they probably can't.

When we picture the life of a butterfly floating from flower to flower, it's hard to believe it has any worries of its own. So is the purity of a "simple life" a sort of bliss? Is it a presentness that each and every one of us humans strives to reach each and every day? Do these insects with their glossy, black marble eyes perhaps have it figured out better than we do? Do they understand the meaning of their little lives—to pollinate, decompose, and protect the queen—more than we humans understand our lives?

Every life, no matter how long or short, and no matter how intelligent its species may be, is rich and complicated and full of all the beauty and terror of what it means to exist. Smallness is merely a matter of perspective. For in each and every ant, caterpillar, and roly-poly crawling through spring blooms and hiding under wet logs, there lies the essence of the entire universe.

Diary Entry from a Seven-Day-Old Ant

**Note: Please read the following entry in the voice of Werner Herzog.*
***Note 2: Please look up a video of Werner talking if you don't know who he is.*

We are small, but we are many. We are many, but we are one. No, not the hive, not the labyrinthian network of tunnels and chambers. I speak only of the ants. I speak only of the we. We march ever onward. We do our work. We look up, questioning the towering, monstrous humans, those pests who decimate our hives, those brutes who set us afire with giant translucent circles bending light itself into death rays. Are those lumbering apes not indeed a hive mind just as we are? They, who build cities together and live in stacks atop one another, who walk and drive in little lines through their own colonies. They speak of individuality and adorn themselves with colored garbs and fanciful phrases like "Just do it" and "I'm with stupid." They decorate their lives with things: pickup trucks, disco balls, chocolate bars. How small these things are in the grand scheme of things; how puny they are in comparison to us. Do they not see that they, too, are bound to each other? Do they not watch themselves building a society and a culture, learning from one another in every moment? In all their desperate attempts to separate themselves, to rise above or to run away, can they not see that we living things are supposed to work together? Do they not see how wonderful it is to be part of a we?

Anyway, this week's been pretty good. I found a jelly bean. It was humongous. Me and all the guys were chowing down.

TTYL.
—Ant #412,312,352 (Franz)

FRANZ

Fungi

One single, quiet, lonely mushroom pokes its cap through the wet, mossy soil. A small gust of wind blows over and underneath the cap, causing its fishlike gills to release a fine bluish powder: spores. It is weird, alien perhaps, but somehow beautiful. Even though it seems like this fungus is from another world, it could not be more at home. If you trace your finger through the soil beneath the mushroom's stem, a wispy, white web of mycelium is revealed, connecting the solitary mushroom to so much more. Looking close, you see a million tiny separate things, but if you look closer still, you might realize that nothing is really separate.

Hidden beneath the calm forest floor lies the hustle and bustle of an entire city. The mycelial body functions as a network of tendrils that navigate their way from tree to tree, only breaking through the soil to release its spores and fruit. Although it's not easily visible, a world of connection and quiet communication exists beneath your very feet. Through this network, a beautiful exchange of goods and services takes place, with currency in the form of nutrients, energy, and information. Trees provide mycelium with sugars from the sun, while mycelium provide trees with moisture and minerals from depths below the trees' roots. Through their symbiotic relationship with the web of fungi, referred to as the mycorrhizal network, the trees themselves transfer energy, resources, and warnings of potential threats to each other. Beneath the roots, it's obvious: The fundamental force of life is connection. But all we ever see of these beautiful mycorrhizal connections are the little mushroom caps peeking out of the ground.

Stepping outside onto the sidewalks in our neighborhoods, we walk around our own interconnected webs of tendrils weaving through our cities. We are connected—neighbor to neighbor, stranger to stranger, all of us relying on and communicating with each other like the inhabitants of the forest floor. Roads and railways wind routes between us, bringing us closer together; telephone wires, the internet, and mail trucks all do their jobs, exchanging information across long distances; drinking water miraculously flows underneath our homes to our faucets; food arrives at the market right on time; and garbage disappears weekly from our full bins. It's easy to take all this for granted, but we have to remember that this is the result of countless people building, maintaining, and working together to help each other: bakers, sanitation workers, mail carriers, construction workers, and bus drivers. Whether we realize it or not, we are doing things for each other, and for the greater good, all the time. If you look at our not-so-distant forest-dwelling cousins, you can see why. The amazing interconnectedness of mycelium isn't a strange miracle—it is nature. Caring for one another and helping each other thrive is *human nature*. It's as simple as a neighbor lending you a cup of sugar, or a stranger on the subway during your daily commute becoming a friend. You give, you take, and you grow toward love, all with a common purpose.

You get to choose how you want to be connected with the world around you. Perhaps you receive love when the time is right, growing small on the underside of a mossy log, appreciated only by the experienced forager. Or perhaps you are the forager who finds a glorious oyster mushroom growing proudly on the side of a decaying tree, ready to be appreciated, taken home, seasoned with salt and pepper, and sautéed. Both you and the mushroom are tiny parts of something much bigger—a system of nourishing and being nourished, of finding and being found.

You get to choose how you want to be connected with the world around you.

From Rain, Back to Mud

Picture the endless chain of events that led to the single raindrop that fell out of the sky and landed on the tip of your nose. It might start off like this:

More than a thousand feet in the air, in the shadowy pillar of a cumulus cloud, a tiny dust particle dances with random gusts of air. It is getting colder. Little by little, the invisible water vapor in the air makes a fantastical transformation, changing forms from floating gas to shimmering liquid, condensing on the microscopic surface of the particulate. The water clings to the tiny speck, getting wetter and heavier every second.

Think of the millions of things that had to happen in the exact way they did for this one particle to be exactly where it is, suspended in the air, blown in every direction by cold and hot air. As the invisible air cools and water forms on its surface, think of all the things that have happened to make the world you see around you.

As sublime as the process that turns air into water is, every occurrence—from supernovas to lines at the airport—comes into being because of an unbelievable chain of events so long and improbable (and interwoven with everything else) that it would be impossible to ever untangle it. Endless particles knock together, moving as conditions change. One particle does this, another does that, and the entropy continues to swirl. This connection of events is so knotted up and hard to understand that maybe we shouldn't even think of it as a chain at all. Maybe it is better to think of it as a cloud.

The cloud of everything that has ever happened and ever could happen floats in the air. Every event, every tiny change, buzzes and bumps around the cloud in an endless random dance. This. Then. That. Then. That. Only when the prevailing winds blow just right and the temperature shifts in the ideal direction with the necessary particles located in the perfect spot—only then does something really start to happen.

A tiny speck—dust or dirt or soot—gathers water from the cooling air. It gets heavier, and wetter. Suddenly, when enough water has clung to it, when the floating ocean gets too heavy to drift along, Earth calls to it from below, begging it to fall. Down through the cloud of possibility and cause and effect, down from the history of the whole planet that has come before. It falls out of the gray cloud in just the right way, emerging into open air. Finally, it is rain. Finally, each thing becomes what it is.

It is a normal day. The sun rises. The ants crawl along the dirt at the base of a tree. A cloud floats more than a thousand feet overhead. The dirt is dry.

But a drop of rain is falling, put together by countless atoms gathering at random, moving toward Earth through the strangeness of three-dimensional space, moving through time, each second like an eternity. This one drop will change everything.

The drop of rain lands, slamming into the dirt and leaving a small, dewy crater. Another lands. And then another. And another. The earth comes alive. The dirt drinks in the water, waking the teeming microscopic lives inside it, thirsty and wild, as worms wriggle to the surface.

Every question we have asked so far in regard to life, space, time, and perception hangs in the air high above our heads. What is all this? Where does it come from? How does it work? Where do we fit in?

The answers, as it just so happens, come as a chorus of little splats, a thousand raindrops hitting the ground. The rain and the dirt do not have the full answers—but here, an inch from the ground, you can see that the journey to finding these answers is before you. Allow yourself to see, and smell, and hear how rich and alive the mystery really is.

The rain is not rain anymore. The dirt is not dirt. By coming together and sharing different pieces of themselves, they have both become something new.

Now, there is mud.

What is all this?
Where does it come from?
How does it work?
Where do we fit in?

INDIVID

UAL

O to 1

When you break a rock in half
and throw away one side,
what are you holding?

The half,
or the new whole?

You might say both,
or you might say neither,
or you might think it is a stupid question,
and you're probably right.

But when an ancient redwood falls,
you might see tragedy.
You might see something going from 1 to 0,
but come back in a thousand years,
and you'll count six trees
sprouting skyward in a ring.

When a seed rests in your open palm,
what is it you are holding?

This one seed,
or the whole forest?
The green-golden light,
the squirrels darting through the canopy,
the worms wriggling around the roots,
that will grow from
this very seed.

What is the difference
between something
and nothing?

0 to 1,
that widest of chasms
crossed by our humblest integer.

And from it,
the universe and you,
the puzzle and all the pieces.

Everything in one.

One Leaf

Where are we? What is all this stuff made of? What can we depend on besides what we're seeing this very second? And what is a second? What is seeing? *What is anything?* Worst of all: Why?

In facing these big questions, the world can start to feel like a very scary, confusing place. But while we ponder our existence, something is happening beneath our feet. In the darkness of the earth, an inch or two beneath the surface, a seed sits in damp soil while an invisible clock silently ticks. As we lose our grasp of the world and threaten to tumble into complete nonsense, something springs up out of the dark dirt to catch us: a single green leaf. Suddenly, it all becomes so simple. Here is a life: so brilliant, so plain.

Each leaf you see springing out of a crack in the sidewalk is a new life bursting forth. It is common, but that doesn't mean we shouldn't pay attention. All you have to do to fully appreciate this new life is get on your hands and knees and put your face really close to this brand-new plant growing out of the earth. Force yourself to *really* see it: the fledgling stem burrowing through the loose soil and the velvet-soft blade of the first leaf pulling open. In the face of all these major questions—in the face of "What is space? What is time? Why is any of this?"—look down and see the certainty with which this new plant reaches up toward the sun. With so many unanswerable questions, sometimes it's helpful to know that something just is.

Each leaf you see springing out of a crack in the sidewalk is a new life bursting forth.

Sour Grass

Observe a single piece of sour grass. Examine it as if you are a bacterium latching on to its cloverlike leaves, or imagine you are a plant cell inside of it, holding together the rigid cellulose structure that's tasked with photosynthesis. Or perhaps envision that you are an ant crawling on its leaf, gazing up at the rays of light refracting through the dewy droplets brought on by the marine layer, your antennae smelling the sour-sweetness of the glucose encased in the stem, just beyond the cell wall. Or imagine yourself on a hike, trekking past rows and rows of sour grass lining the trail. What a joyous sight. Look at the clover shape and think: *This must mean something.*

You reach into the sour grass, careful not to disturb an ant enjoying the refracting light, and pick one from the base, stick the stem between your two front teeth, and chew, testing for flavor. You pick a handful to take with you and continue on your way, a satisfying sourness bursting across your taste buds with every chew. You spit out the fibrous remains when you're done, an offering for the banana slugs.

Imagine you are a redwood tree next to a shaded creek that's quickly flowing, where rays of sun stream through your branches, stippling the sour grass decorating the base of your trunk with dappled light. You can feel the sour grass collect and store moisture, sharing it with your roots. The sour grass is your friend, a fellow photosynthesizer. Looking down on it from your towering canopy, the sour grass might look small, but from the perspective of your roots, it might look like another tree, reaching for the sky.

No matter how you look at it, this one sprout of sour grass, tiny as it may appear, is actually enormous. It is alive and full of purpose and meaning. An ant sees it as a skyscraper, and a bacterium sees it as the whole universe. On its own, it is endless potential and priceless beauty. It lives in a kind of utopia, with the sun, nutrient-rich soil, and dew running down to its roots. It has everything it needs, an admirable simplicity to its very existence. It grows in symbiosis with the world around it. Utopia might sound far-fetched, but maybe it isn't so far-off.

You, too, are like the sour grass. You are part of a connected cycle that provides the simple necessities of life—sun, food, water, and beauty to appreciate. Each life is a purpose in itself. We exist in this utopia: a symbiosis and mutual connection between everything, and take it for granted every day. Yes, the world is far from perfect, but maybe life itself is a utopia of its own creation.

The World's Largest Tree

The coastal redwood tree (*sequoia sempervirens*) that grows in California is one of the largest living organisms on the planet. If you've never seen one in real life, it's kind of hard to understand the feeling that comes over you when you look up at the enormous living thing towering high into the sky.

Every tree is beautiful: the humble roots burrowing into the soil and drinking in the earth; the trunk reaching upward, strong and steadfast; and the shocking, brilliant green leaves reaching out like open hands, catching the sunlight and bringing energy and shelter to the world below. Every tree is a microcosm of life, a branching, far-reaching symbol for the story of evolution. Each tree is a miracle of its own. But when you walk up to a redwood for the first time, you might wonder if you have ever actually seen a tree before.

From far away, you might not make too much of it. It's a coniferous tree with a shape not too different from what you've seen before. It has a straight trunk that shoots up and branches at the top that reach out on all sides, full of green needles. Yet as you get closer, its astounding size becomes clearer. Standing at the foot of a redwood, you will notice a lot. The massive trunk is so large you can't reach around it even if you link hands with ten of your friends. Its unbelievable height reaches so high into the canopy above that you can't see if it ever tapers to a point. It appears so powerful and dominant in its form that your brain might start to compare it to other large things: *This is like a mountain, a giant, or a skyscraper.* But no, none of these comparisons will do. This tree is not like some other thing. This tree is *alive* and cannot be contained by a metaphor.

The giant roots ripple through the loamy ground beneath your feet. As you touch the tree's bark, you may be surprised to find that it's fuzzy—the soft texture akin to felt or velvet, and like a sodden sponge when wet. As you look up, the vibrant green of the canopy overhead shines in your eyes, as you squint and try to catch a glimpse of the treetop, only to fail. The stunning glittering greens above are like a separate world, forever out of reach, which contrast against the stark reddish-browns and blacks of the trunk, casting darkness on the ground below. You will notice all of these things, but more than anything, you will notice the tree's immense presence.

While you stand there with a real-life giant towering over you and the earthy scent of redwood loam filling your nose, there is an overwhelming, unmistakable sensation of the tree's power radiating

The stunning, glittering greens above are like a separate world, forever out of reach . . .

all around you. Here is something far greater than you, and far older. It has been standing, rooted in this exact spot for two thousand years or more, and it will likely still be standing here long after you're gone. To each one of us, our own life feels giant, as we experience everything from our own limited perspectives—our thoughts are massive, our problems dire. Yet here, standing on the soft earth of the forest, you stare at a tree so old that it could hold your entire life in its own, a hundred times over, and your body, a thousand times or more. Here is something, erupting from the damp ground, that takes your whole life and puts it into alignment with the reality of how things really are.

You are so completely small. You are so entirely young. You are so new on this planet. This might be startling to come to terms with, but it is the truth of each of our lives. As the tree tells you these big and small things, you might be frightened by these truths. But we promise you, there is no need to be scared. Standing at the foot of this giant, looking at the red, felt-like bark and hearing the birds flying above in the canopy, you do not feel its presence as an ancient monster towering over you. Instead, you feel the gentle indifference of a very, very old friend. You feel a quiet, steady greeting from something far greater than yourself.

If you've never stood beneath a redwood, you should. But this feeling doesn't emanate from ancient wood and leaves alone. There will always be something much bigger than you, something far older and farther reaching. The setting sun, the raging winds, the twinkling of stars long gone—the entire world is an ancient friend waving hello.

Decomposition

A violent act occurs during a winter storm in the Santa Cruz Mountains in early January. After a dry summer, the intense rain batters the redwood soil, turning the strong structural foundation into soupy mud. Exposed roots attempt to tether themselves, but the winds and the rain are stronger. A redwood tree falls with an unimaginably loud, squealing crash.

The next day, we discover the fallen giant, toppled along one of our favorite trails. It feels almost painful to see the tree in such a state, with collapsed, giant branches split open beneath it.

"This is terrible," I say.

"I know." Thomas shuffles his feet, which squish in the mud.

We're standing in the full midday sun, where there once was only shade. The sun reflects off the leaves, showing a greenery full of life and moisture, but it also reveals a gruesome act. We stare at the foot of the tree. The roots are exposed, and it feels like we're looking into the mouth of an octopus, tendrils flayed and torn from the ground, clumps of wet mud still attached to the ends. One towering gentle giant has fallen and sent shockwaves through the forest floor. Everything and everyone in the forest has felt it. I feel it too.

"This was my favorite tree," I say.

"Really?" Thomas seems confused. "You've never mentioned it before now."

"I never paid it as much attention before," I respond. "But now that it's gone, I realize how much I always loved it without even thinking about it."

"I know what you mean." Thomas nods and looks at the branches reaching up toward the sky. A blue jay screeches as it pecks for something in the forest. "But look." Thomas points at the birds hopping through the branches. "It isn't really gone. It's still here. It's still a part of the forest."

I nod, and we keep walking. I look over my shoulder at the tree, once we have made it farther down the trail. I'd like to think Thomas is right, but I'm not so sure. The toppled tree looks so jagged—so wrong in a forest that looks so right. So dead in a place that is so alive.

Months pass, and the tree still lies where it landed. Creatures of all kinds find little hideaways in this new feature of the forest floor. Birds build nests, bees find hollows for their hives, and the decomposers begin their slow, steady work. Fungi, insects, and invertebrates begin to nibble on the bark and exposed wood. In the path of the tree's fall,

One towering gentle giant has fallen...
and sent shockwaves through the forest floor.

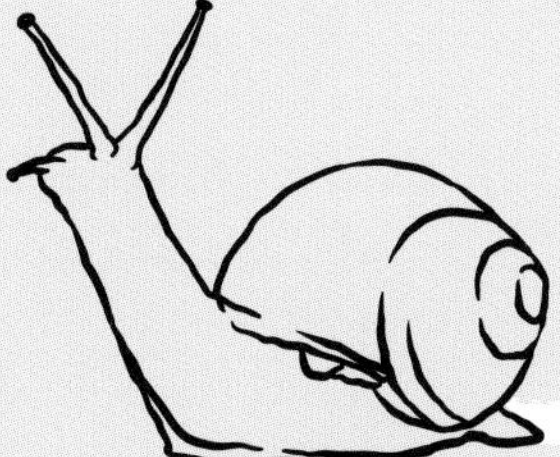

smaller trees take advantage of what has changed: Young redwoods, oaks, and bays drink in the newly available sunlight, growing faster than they have in their entire lives.

The seasons change. Rain falls all spring. Summer is dry. Fall is warmer than usual. Winter brings the rain again.

The tree, once strong, straight, and full of life, slowly softens and bends to the will of gravity over the uneven ground. The decomposers continue their work, as the hard wood softens. Worms, snails, and fungi eat away the moist, spongy wood from the inside.

Mycelium races with its spindles and tendrils through the body of the tree, also eating its way through, producing a beautiful bright-white oyster mushroom to decorate the fallen trunk. Newts squirm with their slippery bodies under the decomposing trunk, the heavy, wet wood becoming a sensation of security and warmth—a home. Day in and day out, the tree lies, slowly being taken in by all the living things around it.

Another year or so later, we walk by and see the tree again. I stand still, looking at the fallen tree and remembering. Its branches are dried and covered in moss and lichen. Its thick trunk has been half swallowed by a mass of blackberry and poison oak. The birds hide and dart from hollow to hollow. I inhale. The smell is wet, earthy, and herbaceous.

"Look at how much it's changed," I say quietly.

"I know," Thomas says. "Look at how much it's doing for all the other life around it."

I see what he means. Even though the tree has been ripped from the ground for more than two years, it looks far from dead. In fact, it looks greener than it ever did, as the leaves and moss spring up all around it.

"You know what I just realized?" I ask. Thomas looks over at me. I say what I'm thinking, and I mean it. "This is still my favorite tree."

I wish I could say we returned the next year, and that an equally beautiful, wide-trunked redwood was growing from the decomposed soil of the fallen one, but that isn't the sort of time frame trees work with. For the next hundred years, the next two hundred years, the fallen tree will lie where it is, decomposing and being reabsorbed by the world. The rings of its wood, each one a checkpoint of its life, a proud layer of growth, will lose their meaning, slowly becoming one with the dirt.

Long after we are gone, there won't be anything left of my favorite tree, except maybe for a lump in the ground that future hikers might walk upon. Perhaps there will be a small hill composed of the tree's final debris, overlooking a view that a hippie from the future can ponder over. But the energy in that tree will merge into the environment that birthed it, becoming the fertile soil, the stage, and the food for life—new redwoods, ivy, moss, and more. The redwood still is. It is just as living as it once was. In the forest, there is no such thing as gone for good.

A Newt

The morning starts like every morning. In the dark.

On an unassuming patch of the forest floor, there is a small hole in the ground. Beneath the surface, a newt is stirring. The loamy soil surrounding the hole is damp, the earth held together by decomposing trees that retain water like sponges to conserve moisture. Mosses, fungi, lichen, and other green things thrive in this damp, beautiful microcosm. And then, when the time is right, from the darkness a slimy nose pokes out of the soil. Two marble-like eyes blink in the sun.

No, it's too sunny. Not safe, I must go back in.

The sun rises higher in the sky, keeping the newt in his place. A sheet of marine fog rolls into the forest, bringing with it a cool drizzle.

That sound. That smell. Something is changing.

Then the newt finds the courage to fully emerge from his hole. Tiny, webbed feet reach out, a bright-orange belly and lumpy brown back come into view, as the newt is filled with unrivaled joy, basking in the beauty of this wet, foggy world. He must stay in a constant state of dampness to keep his body from drying up, so it is only now, during the rainy spell, that the newt can experience the world outside his den. He runs, slapping his splayed feet onto the mud, in search of bugs, slugs, or juicy worms—any would make for a fine meal after such a long nap hidden in the earth. Since he is camouflaged among the scattered oak leaves, the newt is able to avoid capture by snakes and other predators. What does a newt think as it stomps its way through the undergrowth?

I am hungry. It is damp. I smell bugs.

Maybe it doesn't think anything at all. Maybe it is perfectly content simply existing.

I am in my right place. I am doing exactly what I am supposed to be doing.

Think of your own life. Think of yourself, driven every day by hunger, instinct, and fear. Like the rough-skinned newt, we spend so much of our time on our own, doing the little things that sustain us. There is a simple joy in it. But for both us and the newts, a solitary life can take you only so far. One day, the newt gets a feeling.

I have to go somewhere. I began in the water as an egg, a larva, and now I must return. It is the right thing to do. It is the only thing to do.

The little amphibian begins his long migration back to the pond where he hatched miles away. This is not a small journey for a newt no bigger than your index finger, but he goes anyway. Fighting his way through tall grasses, he travels farther from his burrow than he has in months. He will have to evade the garter snake—the only predator resistant to the newt's potent toxin—and confront new dangers.

You may be wondering how such a small, simple creature could possibly make such a daunting voyage. As the newt approaches the edge of the foliage, ready to cross a trail, he might even stop to contemplate what we all think when facing adversity.

I've done this before. I'll do it again.

Then, the newt sees a red-brown shape moving through the grass beside him. And then another, and another. All the other newts are making the same migration. He recognizes them, and remembers.

We've done this before. We all have. We'll do this the only way we can. Together.

The newts waddle their way back to the pond like they always do, once a year. Though small, these rough-skinned newts can live for as long as twenty-five years, making the same journey every spring. Though they are usually solitary creatures, during their migrations the newts walk together.

Yes, we humans have more complex lives than our amphibious friends, but we also have a lot in common. You might think it's strange to call such simple creatures wise, but it is clear they recognize something we often forget about when facing a harsh world. When we want to go our farthest or confront our greatest obstacles, we have to walk together.

Hey, man!

The Forest of Self

This is a forest—
your body, head, and mind.
I'm sorry for all the worry,
the shadows, thickets, and thorns,
but this forest of self,
I imagine, has a sky
and a ground, and
I think it might be
home to a damp newt
hiding in the pine needles.
And maybe that's the real us.

The salamander might look up
and smell the air, predicting rain,
and we might be right.

The laughing rain might
come and wash us,
as silly rocks tumble through streams,
and moss wakes up and thanks
the day for being here again.

We might watch the trees
sway and the clouds toil,
but they are not what we are.

They are only
a landscape to play in,
feeding and teaching
the shy creature
all it can.

We might lift our heads
from the loamy ground,
and remember what
a forest is really for.

Like a Bird

In the stillness of the morning, when the wind and rain cease, the quietness is so loud you can hear a needle drop. Then, one singular caw, then a chirp, then a cacophony of sounds as an orchestra of birdsong awakens. Birds of all shapes and sizes, having migrated from different lands over vast oceans, over cities, and over us have come together to harmonize this dawn chorus. It sounds so beautiful. Do they realize how lovely their song is? And more importantly, why are they singing at all?

Maybe the birds are singing to attract a mate, to demonstrate dominance, or to warn others of predators in the area. Or maybe some deeper part of these birds knows how beautiful their music-making is. Their song echoes, filling the spaces between the forest trees—or the buildings that populate our cities—with color and life. Maybe these birds sing not because they have to but because they want to. Perhaps they are simply expressing their will to live.

When you consider a bird like a night heron, it may appear to be a strange dinosaur-like creature swimming through the evening fog, searching the marshlands for fish to bring back to its babies. Its call makes a cracking that sounds like something from a construction site—loud and rattling, similar to the noise a jackhammer makes. Then there's the woodpecker, with its alien biology: a chisel for a beak and a tongue that wraps around its very skull. It is made for drilling holes into the oakwood, its body parts meticulously sized to access the acorns they need to gather and store for the winter months. Think of the simple crow, a bird that is beautifully intelligent, with a black coat of waxy feathers. It is sleek and aerodynamic and has the ability to recognize human faces and solve complex puzzles.

Watching them circle high overhead, you might get the feeling that they understand some things we don't. Maybe they understand the *whole* more than we do. How insignificant we must be to them,

as they fly above us every day. To a bird, a city is but an obstacle to fly around. They stare down at us where we toil on the ground. With a bird's-eye view of everything going on, they might be bewildered by the sight of humans below in their cars, stuck and unmoving, caught in traffic on the freeways. *What absurd inefficiency*, they must think, *that these humans constantly contain themselves in such small boxes. What are they even doing down there? Why do they live in such small spaces? Why can't they spread their wings?*

The confusion goes both ways, as humans look up, amazed by how freely birds move through the world. We do not understand fully why birds migrate. If a migratory bird is caged in the spring or fall, it will become restless and flutter repeatedly to one side of the cage, unable to quell its urge to migrate. We do not know how they find their winter homes, why they choose particular locations over others, or how they are able to miraculously return each spring to the place where they were born. Perhaps even birds do not understand—they don't think; they just do. Birds cover thousands of miles in flight, often putting themselves through intense physical stress and increased potential harm from predators, just to reach the place that somehow intrinsically calls to them, as if written on their bones. Why do they take these risks?

While we measure our accomplishments with gold stars, lollipops, and money, a bird does quite the opposite. Looking down from high above, it can see how small those things really are. It carries nothing, yet it has everything it needs. The bird has faith that the winds will guide them in the right direction, that the sky will always be there to carry them. To a bird, the world as a whole is their home. Maybe they are right: Life isn't for holding on to things but for how we choose to glide through it, navigating the wind currents and figuring out how to sing while doing it.

You get a feeling
and you start swimming.

You Are a Fish

In the frigid waters of a glacial river, unencumbered by the daily fears of a human, you swim. You are unaware that you need water to live, unaware that you are even in something that is called *water* to begin with. For you, the concept of water is intrinsic—it is your entire universe. It is a universe of currents, algae, and unfathomable depths and reason that land dwellers could never understand.

You are swimming against the massive weight of the current, pushing past all the odds stacked against you. There is a goal, and even though you might not understand what it is, you know with certainty that you are headed in the right direction.

You swim past the ancient Douglas firs and spruces growing along the river's shores, underneath the iridescent flies resting atop the water, through meticulously crafted lures strewn out by eager fishermen, past behemoth mammalian monsters that reach at you with pointed claws and sharp teeth. You should be scared, but you are not. You are a fish, a fish that swims upstream.

Why do you swim this way? It isn't easy, but it is right. It is good. This you know. It is something written into your every shining scale, which glisten as you swim, just as it is written into every ripple running on the surface above you. *Go that way*, it says. How do you know? How does anyone know what they are supposed to do? You get a feeling and you start swimming. And even if you don't know whether the journey upriver will make a difference in the long run, if it will take you to a turquoise lake or the open sea, you know the pursuit, the swimming itself, is more than worth the struggle. The cool water rushing by every instant, the green ferns arching above you, and the feeling in your bones that you are doing what you are meant to do: this is why we swim upstream.

A Good Squirrel

A squirrel is nibbling on the corner of a discarded Dorito in the tree overhead. I watch him intently. He holds the chip like he is eating pizza. His face is covered in cool-ranch powder. He notices me watching and circles the tree twice, then darts into a little hole. It makes me wonder.

"Hey, man, what is a good squirrel?" I ask.

The squirrel chatters and hops through the branches of the oak tree above us.

"What?" Thomas replies, distracted.

"Like, what makes a squirrel . . . good?"

Thomas strokes his chin like we are considering something very important. He takes on the character and voice of a professor of philosophy. "Hmm . . . I'm glad you brought this up. There is much to discuss."

I grin and stand up as if I am Socrates and it's time to deliver my monologue. I begin pacing back and forth. "Is the goodness of a squirrel measured by how many acorns it can store in its cheeks? How many it can store in a little den for hibernation in the winter? Certainly, this would be a very successful squirrel, but does success a good squirrel make?"

Thomas shakes his head and retorts in a gruff voice. "Well, obviously not. A squirrel's goodness isn't measured by all that it's achieved. Though the squirrel may in turn be healthier and less driven by the dangers of hunger, a greater darkness could be at play."

I bellow, emphatically raising a fist, "Do tell!"

"Perhaps the drive to hoard acorns is the product of a deep-seated selfishness. Should not the fruitful riches of an oak tree be shared with every squirrel? Would not a good squirrel know this?"

"Preposterous!" I shout back. "You're applying morals to a forest critter. It's only doing what a squirrel must do! Isn't a good squirrel the one who does its best job of living the most squirrel-like life?"

"Maybe. The squirrel is doing its job, isn't it?"

"But didn't humans define that as well? We project the idea of what a squirrel should be onto every squirrel we see. I'm asking what makes a squirrel extraordinary."

Thomas leaps to his feet in a fit of joy. "Ahh! So maybe it's the squirrel that doesn't fit inside the idea, like the squirrel last week that brought me a dandelion in exchange for a peanut. That squirrel left an impact because it did something beyond "the squirrel."

Thomas lowers his air quotes.

"Eureka! That's it!" I exclaim. "The squirrel that lives outside the box, that strives to be more than just the animal instinct. That is the good squirrel. The cream of the critter crop!"

"Hmm. But does that mean the rest of the squirrels are bad? That just isn't true. I think we have once again mistaken greatness for goodness. A classic foible! Our understanding of good has to be simpler than that."

I look up to see the Dorito-faced squirrel climbing higher into the oak tree. "Well, maybe every squirrel is good . . ."

"That can't be it. There's gotta be evil ones."

"There might be. But is it the squirrel's fault that it is that way? Each squirrel comes into the world without any control over the situation it's coming into. All it can do is try to find its way from there. Doesn't every squirrel start out good?

"Yeah, I guess it does," Thomas says quietly.

"So no matter what mistakes a squirrel makes, on some level there is still that goodness in it worth appreciating?"

"Yeah, I guess there is. Maybe every squirrel *is* a good squirrel."

I sit back down. The academic lecture is over. A Dorito crumb falls from somewhere high up in the tree.

The Mountain Lion

My long day in the sun is almost over.
The path veers into the deep valley,
the sun has passed behind that distant hill.

Dusk has found me
on my two feet, hiking on the ridge
I have known all my life.
But even here, in the seat of my life's joy,
in the rich green of late spring,
I feel it.

Invisible eyes watching
the soft parts of my neck,
hiding in a hollow of the boulder
or crouching poised in the thicket
beneath the granary oak.
The big cat who goes by so
many names lies in wait.
The puma, the cougar,
the mountain screamer,
the only monster my parents
ever told me to be afraid of.

Call it a trick of the mind
or the shadow of a tree swaying just right,
but sometimes in the most remote corners,
when the dusk catches you in
its purple-velvet quiet,
you know you are not alone.
The only name the body knows
for this is fear.

There is that strange bargaining
of the naturalist,
servile to the law that
what is natural must be right.

Without the puma, the balance dies:
the forests chewed bare by deer,
the birds unfed, the rivers unclean.

But here, in the crosshairs
of the darkening forest,
I find no more comfort
in the beauty of ecology
than the buck felled by the sinking
in of one or two perfect teeth.

But, still,
no screaming death leaps
out to drag me away.
The dim blue dusk hangs in the leaves,
and I walk the rest of the trail,
quite perfectly safe,
watching for the reckoning
that may never come.

The trees rise up around me,
the night birds begin to call,
and the river runs clear through
the valley, into the dark.

The only law by which nature abides:
What can happen must happen.
To survive, each thing must survive.

I don't know how
to hate it,
or how to love it,
but somewhere in the darkness,
the mountain lion drinks.

Fear for a Deer

A deer stands frozen at the edge of a clearing. Its damp black nose gently puffs shallow breaths of warm air into the cold morning, as its tawny coat blends into the dry grass beneath it. With narrow two-pronged hooves standing lightly on the ground, the deer trembles ever so slightly in anticipation, ready to escape if needed, at any instant. The deer's two shining eyes, like black marbles, stare out into the wide world that surrounds it. The deer is afraid.

This is what a deer does when it hears a twig snap or when it sees a shadow move in the corner of its impossibly wide field of view. It freezes in place, opens its eyes wider, and raises its ears to take in as much information as possible. Through evolution, the deer has adapted to camouflage itself from danger. It wants to be invisible, to attract the least attention possible from any creature passing by, and take up as little space as it can. If it could, the deer might shrink until it vanishes completely.

We all know this feeling. We want to be safe, to disappear. Some of us might know this feeling all too well.

Standing alone in the clearing, while the morning dew still clings to each blade of grass, the deer asks the world, *Am I in danger? If so, how much and how soon?* Then the world gives an answer.

We might not walk through the woods on high alert for predators around every corner, but we are still animals. We have the same instincts our ancestors did when they were on watch for saber-toothed tigers hiding in the bushes. Although a lot has changed since then, we still get scared. When something unexpected happens, when danger presents itself, when some great unknown looms large over our heads—we have the same reaction. We tense, freeze, and then prepare ourselves to spring into action.

If nothing happens after the deer is first alerted to potential danger, it might relax and return to the grass it was nibbling on. But if the disrupting sound gets louder, if the distant movement gets nearer, if the unknown possibilities grow too large, the deer knows what it has to do. It does what its body has adapted to do over millions of years and countless generations: It runs.

Like a bolt of lightning, the deer snaps into action, from perfect stillness to adept motion, leaping and flying between the oak trees, vanishing from view in less than a moment to find another safe place where it can rest. For the deer, it is simple. Fear is not a bad thing. It is a tool. It is what lets the deer continue to be a deer. The instincts to freeze and run are just as much part of the deer's life as is the instinct to find an acorn on the ground to eat.

Why should we be any different? Our fear should exist only as a fleeting instinct that exists to ensure our survival: arising, being addressed, and then fading away. Unfortunately, for so many of us, fear is not merely a passing experience. Even if it doesn't consume our lives, our fear is often more concerning than a moment of caution between nibbling acorns.

The main difference between how a deer experiences fear and how we do is that the things we are afraid of are not always so immediate as a mountain lion crouching in tall grass. We are thinking animals that take in information and extrapolate, constantly trying to predict what is coming, imagining what might be possible, and taking the necessary steps to prepare for whatever may come. So often, the things we are afraid of are bigger, more abstract, and don't appear for months or years after we first become afraid, if they ever reveal themselves at all. We are afraid of the future

and the unknown, and what's more, we are afraid of all the complex emotions that simmer inside us. These aren't things we can easily fight off or run away from. Instead of reacting to our fright and finding relief, we can get stuck in the moment of fear, frozen in place.

Maybe this is why, for so many of us, the very experience of our lives seems to be a negotiation with fear. It's why our days are arranged by it, numbered by it, why our entire lives can be swallowed by it. We can become trapped in the instant of crisis, desperately scanning our surroundings, searching our minds, and calculating probabilities. We become like the eager deer, trembling in the morning dew. We are always ready to run, but we never start running, because we can't run from our own minds. So, we ask the world, *Am I in danger? How much and how soon?* And usually, we don't get an answer, so the fear grows, and the wilderness of our minds gives us no place to rest.

Are we missing something? Is there something the humble deer knows that we don't? What is it the deer understands that tells it to relax and go back to chewing on the damp morning grass? What tells the deer the sound it heard was only the falling of a branch? The answer, if we had to guess, is no answer at all. It is only silence that tells the deer there is nothing to fear. When it raises its ears, opens its eyes wide, and witnesses only the continued quiet of the day beginning, it lets its fear go.

Maybe, if we can learn to listen for that emptiness, if we can find calm in the nothingness that answers our concerns when we ask what is wrong, we might start to feel a little less scared.

When an Animal Is Born

When an animal is born,
it knows what to do.

Stumbling out,
legs splayed,
it might look at its paws, hooves,
still damp,
and for one moment
need to think.

Of all the things in the wide world—
mountain lion, crab, cow, mayfly,
and the solemn night heron—
which one will it be
this time around?

Or of course,
it does not have our same curse.

The trembling child tumbles into
the light without questions and sees
the whole world of tickling
incomprehension as what it really is:

A mirror,
or something older—
the dappled reflection on the water,
the gentle pond of this world's self.

It could simply be born,
know it,
and swim.

One Person

Picture a person—any person will do. Picture everything you can about them.

You might think of your mom or dad, just a few rooms over or across the country, going about their day. You might think of an old friend, someone whom you know completely and can tell anything to, and see them smiling to themselves as they make their morning commute. You might picture someone you haven't seen in a very long time. Maybe you used to be close, but you've slowly drifted apart. Or maybe it's someone completely random who just came into your mind. It's funny how thoughts of different people will drift into your head now and then. You're going about your life, and suddenly you're caught wondering what your lab partner from tenth-grade chemistry is doing right now. *Has everything gone how they hoped it would? Do they still like to dance?* You might even picture a complete stranger: someone who passed you on the street carrying a bouquet of flowers, someone you smiled at as you minded your business on the train, or someone driving one of the hundreds of other cars stuck in traffic on your way home—even if none of these people ever saw you. You can picture anyone you wish; just try to imagine them as completely as you can.

Picture their face: What do their nose, eyes, and mouth look like? Think of how their face changes when a smile spreads across their cheeks. How does their laugh sound? Picture them with their family and their childhood friends. Does their laugh change depending on who they're with?

Picture someone you have loved. Picture someone you have hated. Picture the way their eyes move when they wake up in the morning and scan their bedroom. Think about all the decisions they made to put their room together just like that. Why's the bed in the corner? If it's messy, why do you think that is? If it's clean, is it because they spent hours organizing it? Maybe that's just how it is. Picture what that person may be feeling. Imagine what their first thought is as they roll out of bed. Think about where they find the light throughout their days and how they handle the darkness.

Think of their hair and how it falls behind their ears around lunchtime, curling long or cut short. Think of the clothes they wear, the rings on their fingers, and the smoothness of their skin on the underside of their forearms. Imagine the music they hum to themselves in the quiet of the afternoon and the tiredness that grows inside them as they go about their day's work. The worry that things might not get better. The hope that one day everything does.

Picture anyone. Picture anyone in the world this way. Don't you start to *feel* something? Don't you start to *know* something? That anyone and everyone you can possibly imagine—every stranger on the street, and all those you will never meet—is living a life every bit as rich and dripping with meaning, worry, and sweat as yours?

Every individual has an infinity of experiences inside them every single moment, just like you do. Even those people you think you have nothing in common with are living their lives in the only way they know how, just like you are. If you can understand this, even if you know nothing else, you can learn so much more about the people that fill your world, because they are just like you. And if you know this, then maybe you can start to love them, too.

You Are Not Alone

We sit on the top of a hill, watching the cars roll along the highway in the distance. Andy wanted to hike up here to get a good view of the sunset over the ocean, and I tagged along. It is late in the day now, and the highway is full of people heading home, looking quite tiny from this far up. An idea stirs in my head that I have to speak aloud.

"Isn't it weird that everyone is someone? Like, every single person you see in a day is living a life that's just like yours?"

"I guess so . . . " Andy replies, looking at a line of ants crawling along the grass beside him. They march in a perfectly straight line, from some point of interest back to their home. He tilts his head. "But how else is it supposed to be?"

The faint roar of a motorcycle accelerating echoes through the hills. I try to spot the vehicle that goes with the sound, but I can't seem to. "I guess I just mean that in regular life, when you aren't really thinking about it, it doesn't always feel like that," I say. "It's so easy to forget about other people when you're in your own head."

Andy brushes his hands on his jeans and scans the horizon. "It makes sense, though. We're all worried about our own stuff. If we were always thinking about how everyone else has just as much

stuff to worry about as we do, it'd be too much."

"But everyone *does* have just as much stuff to worry about as we do."

"Yeah, they do. But we still have our own lives to focus on."

"But when we only worry about ourselves, everything gets lonelier," I say, still gazing out over the landscape before us. "Going about your day, everyone is just an obstacle, you know? Like the cars blocking your way in traffic. Something to get around, or to get something from."

"I know the feeling," Andy says, agreeing.

"But when you really take the time to think about how everyone else is living a life just like yours, it's different."

"Yeah, instead of getting mad at people, or not even thinking about them at all, you might understand where they're coming from a little bit more. Like, they have worries too."

"Exactly!" I say, my voice getting louder.

"But wouldn't you still be worried? Why use your time and energy to think about it this way?"

"You might still be worried about your stuff, but at least you wouldn't be alone," I reply, working out the reasoning in real time as I speak. "You'd start to see that nobody, not even you, is in this alone. You'd know that everyone in the world is going through it all right alongside you." I watch the ants who are still crawling along the grass. The cars in the distance crawl, too, single file from wherever they were to their homes and back again. "And it's not just worries. Every day, a million wonderful things are happening to people all over the place. Even on a bad day, isn't it good to know that somewhere out in the world, someone is having a good day?"

"I guess you're right," Andy whispers.

The ants are carrying a leaf. The traffic on the highway has cleared up.

When you think of life not as your own solitary experience but as everyone going through life together, your own singular worries become a lot easier to carry, and the opportunities for joy become so much wider.

Because you are not alone. No one is.

Always remember: You are not alone.
No one is.

Surrounding each individual person is an endless web of interrelatedness,

of cause and effect,

of questions asked and answered spreading out in every direction.

Nothing Is Individual

We've been focusing on the individual elements that make up our world. Our goal has been to see what we might learn from each thing while trying to take absolutely nothing for granted. By looking at each isolated part of our world with this sense of wonder, it's possible to learn quite a lot: from the tender simplicity of a newt, to the stunning power of a redwood tree, to the determination of a fish swimming upstream. When you really try to see things individually, you start to notice something.

Everything—from the ants to the mountain lions, from the moss along the river to the lichen growing on a branch a hundred feet in the air—is connected to the world around it. Nothing in this world is truly singular.

When we think about a tiny plant growing in the dirt, we can't help but wonder where that dirt came from. And what about the carbon dioxide it takes in to photosynthesize and build its cell walls? What about the fungus in the ground that affixes nitrogen to make it accessible to plant life? And don't forget about the insects that pollinate seeds. Wouldn't we be missing something if we were to consider only the plant itself without factoring in the wide web of living and nonliving things that give the plant its very life? Maybe, like its own roots or leaves, these elements shouldn't be thought of as loosely connected to the plant, but should instead be understood as common parts of something larger, as parts of the same whole.

We're not just talking about plants either. Surrounding each individual person is an endless web of interrelatedness, of cause and effect, of questions asked and answered spreading out in every direction. Each person is a part of something so much greater than themselves, extending to their family, their friends, their community, and the entire human world. To understand each other—to understand ourselves—we can't think of people merely as disconnected individuals. We have to consider every single person as a part of an interconnected community of being, a community with a shared history, a shared future, and most urgently of all, a shared present.

This might feel like grasping at straws or some far-fetched philosophical way to compare the human world with the natural world. But let us remind you: The human world is part of the natural world, and it is just *one part* of it. And everything that connects to us branches in every direction. We are one tiny part of something much bigger.

When you pay attention to each thing individually, you can't help but notice: Nothing is individual.

Part III
ECOS

YSTEMS

The Tree of Life's Only Law

There is a tree,
and you are on it.

Five hundred million years ago,
you and a brainless jellyfish
floating through the deepest
oceans parted ways.

Some of that drifting primordial ooze
stayed where it was.
Some became human.

There is a spider crawling deftly
in the corner of the room.
There are flowers growing
silently on the hillside.
There is a hermit crab crawling
from lukewarm salty shallows
to the beckoning shore.

Three-point-seven billion years of life.
Five hundred and seventy million years
of plants turning light into sweet energy,
of creatures swimming,
crawling, and writhing
on this Earth,
and in just a few thousand,
we claim to have built the world.

Walls, and stories, and cities,
enough to almost make us forget
we did not come *into* this world
but *from* it.

There is nothing we have built
that has not been given to us
by soil, bone, and green things.

This is what
the whole living planet—
each cell
whirring along in harmony
with every other—
tells us every day.

Nothing does anything on its own;
each living thing owes a debt to all life.

Drink in the sun,
and craft sweetness
you will never taste.

Each leaf grows from one tree.

The Forest

We hike across the wet, green hilltops of the Santa Cruz Mountains, the trees still dripping from the marine layer that enveloped the area the night before. The soil and pine needles we step on are dark and smell of that rich, almost chocolaty earth. The biomes around us change as we make our way down the hills, where the terrain becomes rockier and more rugged and more exposed to the harshness of the sun. Here, the air smells like hay and dried rosemary, or maybe it's oak. We follow the streams of rain, trickling from high on the mountain down to the broad creek. The creek is pristine and lined with ferns, with rays of sunshine illuminating the water like a spotlight, the water glittering like some unknown treasure. Water bugs dance on the creek's surface as vibrant blue crawfish loiter at the bottom, waiting for their prey. Meanwhile, the banana slug—

"Oh shit," Thomas says, cutting off my train of thought.

"What's wrong?"

"I feel like there's something I'm supposed to be doing."

We look at the golden sunrays making their way through the trees, shining on the creek.

"Like what?" I ask.

"I don't know! It just feels like there's something

I'm forgetting. Like I left the stove on, or forgot about a book report I'm supposed to be working on."

"A book report? Dude, you're twenty-four," I say, laughing.

"Yeah, I know. But it's the feeling! Like, I could be starting a small business! Or working on my autobiography!"

We continue walking, and Thomas doesn't look at the forest around us. He looks down at the ground but doesn't seem to see it. I try to pull him out of this funk as I spot something moving around in the trees. "Whoa, a pileated woodpecker! Look!"

The red-crested bird slams its beak into a carefully crafted hole in a nearby tree.

"Oh, yeah, nice," Thomas says half-heartedly. He sounds worried, hardly giving the dazzling red-feathered bird a glance. "We should probably head back. I have to start saving for retirement."

"What?" I ask, confused.

"You know, IRAs and stuff. They say you've gotta start early."

"But we're out *here*!"

"I know, but there's so much else we could be doing!" Thomas says frantically.

"There's *always* something else you could be doing. But if you spend your whole life thinking about what you *could* be doing, you'll never actually *do* anything."

"What do you mean? I'll accomplish a lot!"

"But you won't actually be present in the moment when you do it," I continue. "Like right now—why are we hiking?" The creek is babbling. The redwoods rise far above us on all sides. "Are we hiking just to be able to say we have hiked? Or are we hiking to *hike*?"

"Aren't they the same?"

"I dunno," I say, trying to put my thoughts into words. "Do you listen to music to have listened, or to enjoy the sound in the moment? Do you hang out with friends just to get it over with, or to enjoy the time you spend together? Our best moments aren't when we are trying to get something or be somewhere else, they're when we are existing in the moment, being where we are, actually *living* our lives."

Thomas furrows his brow. "But what about the stuff we don't want to do? Like, what about doing laundry?" he asks.

"Well, what's better, folding the laundry while thinking about how you just want it to be done, or folding your laundry and noticing you like how it feels to fold warm clothes?"

"I see what you mean," Thomas says, starting to look up at the trees. We keep walking with more intent in every step. The creek rounds a bend, and we make our way up and over a wooden bridge. We are well on our way. "Even though it feels like there are a million things you could be doing," Thomas continues, "the one thing you ever actually can do is to be in the *now*."

"Yeah, 'cause it's always now," I say, smiling.

We look around at the forest—to be right here, right now, with all this. The woodpecker continues to hammer at a tree behind us.

"Whoa, I'm really stepping to step right now," Thomas says. I laugh. We walk to walk. We talk to talk. For now, we don't worry about our retirement funds.

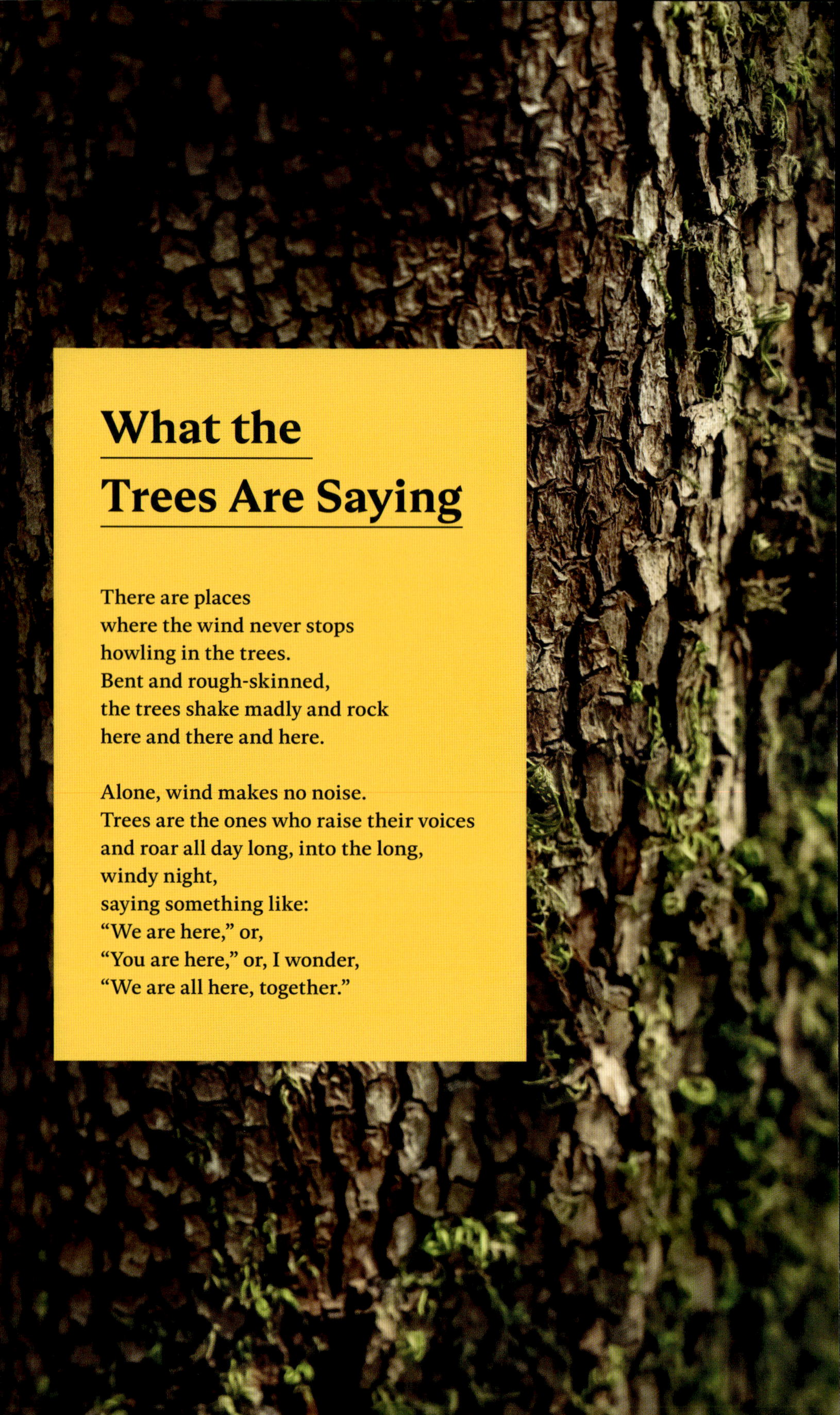

What the Trees Are Saying

There are places
where the wind never stops
howling in the trees.
Bent and rough-skinned,
the trees shake madly and rock
here and there and here.

Alone, wind makes no noise.
Trees are the ones who raise their voices
and roar all day long, into the long,
windy night,
saying something like:
"We are here," or,
"You are here," or, I wonder,
"We are all here, together."

Friends on the Forest Floor

Andy and I lie on our backs underneath a giant, ancient oak tree. We watch the branching dome of spiky leaves sway above us in a gentle wind. It's the time of year when the acorns are falling. Hundreds of green and brown acorns lie all around us in the grass, which sprouts from light-brown dirt. Looking to my right, I see the forest floor stretching out, the acorns like little pieces on a giant checkerboard, with endless ways to play.

Acorns fall into their places. Grass rises up from pebbly soil like tall trees. Ants traverse wide expanses in single file, marching from dusty hole to dusty hole. Pill bugs and darkling beetles scuttle across, careful to avoid the lines of ants. Squirrels dash from their homes in the trees and grab hold of acorns with their handlike paws and chow down, breaking open the hard protective shells to get at the fatty seed core and leaving little piles of scraps and empty acorn husks in their wake. A whole catalog of birds swoops down to the forest floor to do the same. The smaller critters and decomposers work on what is left behind. Fungi, worms, and flies crawl everywhere I look. I can't help but think how well it all seems to work. There is enough food for every living thing I can see, and still there are enough acorns left behind for seeds to take root, for oak saplings to emerge, for the forest to keep growing.

"I wonder if the forest creatures are, like, friends with each other," I wonder aloud.

Andy laughs. "Whoa, dude. That's very Winnie-the-Pooh of you."

I chuckle and then continue. "Don't you think the squirrels and the birds know each other? That they both might feel like the trees are their friends? Like the whole forest—and how well it works—the bugs, the fungi, and the trees, they all take care of each other. Maybe they are friends."

"I think that's a very human way to think about it," Andy says.

We both look at the tree reaching up above us. A gentle breeze shakes some of the last droplets of morning dew from its lowest leaves. I watch as a little circle of water sinks into the soil a few feet from us. A tiny spider crawls along the grass.

"Yeah maybe, but everything is so connected. All the pieces depend on each other," I say.

"Of course they do." Andy shrugs. "They're in the same place at the same time, just trying to survive in a world that's so much bigger than they are. They don't have a choice but to help each other. It's part of being alive."

"Isn't that what friends are? Aren't we all just trying to survive? Don't we make it all easier on each other by making it through together?"

Andy nods in agreement. "Yeah, I guess we do."

Another acorn falls to the ground. Looking out at the forest floor before us and the canopy of trees overhead, it all seems so clear. For a few moments, I see it. All of this—the bugs, the rocks, the acorns, the trees, the squirrel running back to its perch, and the worm hidden deep underground—is united by a kind of friendship. It is something simple in nature, something fundamental to how it all works, and something that unites and cares for all those that are a part of it. We are a part of it too. Everything is.

Ask me on another day, and I might just see a dusty forest floor and some acorns. I might say there's nothing out of the ordinary to see here, and I would be right. But I guess that's the point.

The Circle of All Things

We look around the redwood forest for a moment or two, standing underneath a canopy of towering giants and countless unknown histories, both small and unimaginably large. Maybe there were ancient storms where only the largest redwoods survived; maybe one year the banana slugs were so plentiful they dotted the tree trunks like a yellow-golden glitter and coated the branches with goo. More has happened in this one spot than I could ever understand. Thomas turns to me like he just had a good idea.

"OK, I spy with my little eye, something circular . . ."

"Hmm . . . that's a tough one," I say.

I take note of all the circles around me, but nothing is a perfect circle. Instead, all the things I see are perfect in their imperfection: oblong, oval, and egg-shaped. They're everywhere, from the trunks of wise old oaks to pointy pine cones designed like missiles, meant to fall from treetops down to the ground to foster new growth. I shake my head and make my best guess.

"Redwood tree?" I guess.

"Not quite. Think bigger."

I rack my brain, trying to think of something bigger than the king of the forest. Out of the corner of my eye, I see a slug feasting on a mushroom, which is decomposing a fallen log from an ancient

. . . all the things I see are perfect in their imperfection . . .

redwood tree, feeding the soil to make way for new life. Cycles like these exist alongside all living things and in conjunction with everything else. They help bring about both life and death, in a constant, never-ending exchange. I start to look wider. Fire ants crawl single file on a tree branch, while a brush rabbit shuffles its feet in a patch of poison oak and a red-tailed hawk circles the sky, looking for prey. What does the bunny think of the hawk waiting for it to step out into a clearing, where it might strike? What do the grasses think of the hungry rabbit hopping their way? Do they know their respective roles in this unimaginably complex forest ecosystem? Do they understand how their simple existence helps nourish the community of living things around them every day? Each life is an exchange with the world around it. Each meal is a borrowing, each death a giving back.

"Are you gonna guess again?" Thomas asks.

"Oh right, sorry, man. I got distracted thinking about the cyclical nature of life and death and energy moving between all living things."

"Hmm, and what might you call that?"

I think for a moment. The forest moves with the wind. The ants move along their branch. Do they recognize that each tiny thing they do forever changes the world around them, its effects rippling out into the ecosystem? Did the banana slug eating that one leaf a thousand years ago know it would shape the tree we see today? Do they know that the life they are living was given to them by the many living things that came before? Some part of them must know. Maybe that's what living a life is: doing your best, being connected to everything, and making every choice knowing that what you do, in some little way, changes everything forever. I smile and finally say, "The circle of life?"

"Bingo!" Thomas says with a smile.

Taking energy, being energy, and giving energy back. I think of all the energy flowing through my body right now and picture where it might end up one day. It's a large burden for one slug, or one tree, or one person to bear, sure. Luckily, for all of us, we can bear the weight, together.

"That's definitely not how you play the game, though," I add, laughing.

"Yeah. Sorry," Thomas says sheepishly.

We keep laughing, and continue on our way.

Where Are You?

Where is your mind
as you sit idly on the deck,
looking out at the muddy lake,
as the bugs chirp all day?

Is it in your head
as you scratch your chin
without thinking about it,
and your heart pumps blood
through your body, without asking?

Is it in your eyes
as you look out at the water
folding ten thousand times over itself
in the gentle wind,
watching the clouds drift by
to hide the sun, and then reveal it?

Is it in your body at all,
as the summer day crickets say
a thousand things you know
but don't understand,
as the sun peeks out,
warming the land, and your skin?

As small birds, adept fliers,
dart and skate skyward to places
you will probably never be.

Where is your mind?
Is it in you?
Or is it somewhere far,
so far, out there?

We will find, no doubt,
there isn't much difference.

A River's End

The water roars and ripples, tumbling over rocks, swirling in eddies, carving away the banks, rushing always onward, downhill, toward the sea. We watch the water, ever-changing, and see ourselves in the clear shimmering movement.

Andy and I walk along the river in Anacortes, Washington, making our way on narrow trails through the Pacific Northwest rainforests, stepping over the roots of densely packed cypress trees covered in thick moss. It is summer, and sunlight glistens through the green canopy overhead. The trail meanders away from the water at times, disappearing the river from view, but the roar of it never fades. We turn right and duck through passageways in the leaves, our feet sinking into the decomposing branches on the spongy forest floor. Soon, the tree line ends, and a massive wall of white water comes into view, where a waterfall jumps over a rock ledge and crashes down a warping stone face that's been carved by years of this endless flow.

Andy and I watch the white water tumble into the wide, flat pool below. The ripples emanate from the waterfall, folding the reflection into a thousand concentric rings.

"I wouldn't want to fall in here," Andy eventually says.

"Me neither. That'd probably be . . ." I search for the right word, as the roaring water slams onto the rock with thousands of pounds of force every second.

"Bad?"

"Yeah, it'd be bad," I say, agreeing.

We clamber along the riverbank, hopping over fallen trees on our way down the sloping trail. Underfoot, a pebbly shore replaces solid rock. We get farther from the waterfall, and the roar slowly grows fainter. New sounds replace the white noise. A dragonfly zips over the now-gentle surface of the river. The gurgle of shallow water pours over a fist-size rock into the stillness below. Brown leaves and wisps of green algae circle soundlessly along the river's edge.

"Isn't it weird this is the same water that was in the waterfall?" I ask. "Like, only a second ago it was so intense and scary, and now it's just drifting along, totally calm."

"Well, yeah, what about it?"

I watch a water bug dance along the surface of the flowing water. "It's kind of like us."

"The water?"

"The river," I say, pointing to where the water flows before us.

"What's the difference?"

"That's what I'm wondering. Are we the water or the river?"

"What do you mean?" Andy asks.

If I listen for it, I can hear the roaring of the waterfall in the distance. "If we are like the water, and the river is like our lives, then I guess it means we're flowing through each day. Even though sometimes things are hard, and sometimes things are calm, we don't really change. We always get through it in the end."

"Yeah, I get it."

"But if we're like the river, we always have all that chaos and calm inside us," I say. "We're always changing, carving away at the earth, turning over rocks." I look at the ripples in the river's current. I see myself in the dark reflection. "All a river is, is something that flows a certain way for a certain period of time."

Andy nods deeply and closes his eyes for a moment. "It's just a pattern. After a while, things

change, the land shifts, and the pattern goes away," he says, his eyes still closed.

"Exactly. So which one are we?"

"Huh, I don't know."

Andy manages to skip a rock six times, all the way across the river. Something doesn't feel quite right to me. I hold tightly to a sharp black stone. We walk single file through the warm evening light back to our car at the trailhead. I slip the stone into my pocket.

We decide to drive to the shore of Puget Sound. When we arrive, we take in the water spreading out around us in every direction. The orange-purple of a stunning sunset glistens against every little wave on the Sound's brackish surface. To our right, the mouth of a river opens in a wide, flat spread. The sand and silt cross and braid with small streams as they flow into the expansive sea before us.

"Whoa," Andy exclaims, in awe.

"I know."

We walk over driftwood logs and water-polished rocks, traipsing along the sandy beach. The river water enters the Sound with a gentle gurgle, just barely rippling the saltier body, before mixing in completely, becoming part of the whole. I take the dark rock out of my pocket and point with it toward where the river joins the sea. "I guess it doesn't matter whether we are the river or the water it's made of. The whole time, it is all part of something bigger."

"I guess you're right," Andy replies. "In the end, every drop of water and every river flows into the ocean. It all joins the whole."

The amber-purple haze of the sunset begins to fade as the sun winks behind the horizon. With the last light of dusk glinting on the folding waters, the Sound appears half golden and half black. The river and the water it holds is everything it's ever been before: a storm cloud, a glacier, a waterfall, a gently babbling creek. It is both the river and the water. It is the calm and the fury, both the now and the then.

Here at the end of the river, it becomes something more. Or maybe it comes back to what it was the whole time. Here is where the ocean rejoins itself.

"But if we're the water or the river or whatever, what does that make the ocean?" Andy asks.

"I guess we'll see," I say, not sure how else to reply.

I swing my arm and toss the black stone into the sea, into the place where one becomes all.

The Ocean of Ourselves

It is winter. The beach is cloudy and coated with a crisp blanket of fog. When I look too long at the marine layer drifting through the sky, it's like I can see the whole world around me letting out one long breath. Wind hits my face, like pins and needles on my cheeks. Thomas wants to run into the water, but I am not so sure.

I stare out at the misty ocean and watch the waves move in and out. From far away, they're like mellow moving hills following one after the next, forming whitecaps like mini sailboats in the distance. As they reach the shore, they seem violent and fast-moving, crashing loudly and bubbling into a million whirlpools.

Close or far, the seawater is always moving and changing with the tides. I know there is an entire world swimming in the depths beneath the surface. I wonder, *If I were an ocean, would my whole life be just the waves of my days constantly moving in and out? Are all my everyday joys and worries bubbles on the surface? And if so, what lies beneath the waves of my sea—in the ocean of myself?*

Thomas, eager to dive into the unknown, runs into the water. An enormous wave takes shape, like a creature rising up and roaring. Thomas dives through the center of the wave and comes out the other side. He blows a mist of saltwater out his nose. He cackles and wipes the water from his eyes, then waves and shouts for me to join.

I stare into the horizon. The water—a deep greenish blue—extends endlessly in every direction, making me feel small and scared. There's a whole entire world of its own hidden underneath the water, churning and moving in the darkness.

The fear holds me back. I hover over the water's surface, looking at the frigid crashing waves. It's so beautiful, as the sun's rays peek through the fog, illuminating patches of ocean. It's unreal. How can I dive into the future, into myself, into this wildly unpredictable, chaotic world . . . without knowing what's hidden beneath? Perhaps it's better to stay on the safety of the shore than get stuck out at sea.

In our regular lives, we tend to stay on the safety of the surface, just like this. We think about our day's tasks and our concerns for the coming weeks without considering the big questions. We don't ask ourselves why we're doing what we're doing, why we're living our lives the way we are, or what any of it means, because it's scary to think about these things. If we dive into the big ideas and all the complicated feelings that come with them, it can get dark quickly. It can feel like we're getting pulled under. But if we ignore the depths, we're missing something important. If we only watch the water splashing from the shore, we won't experience the joys of swimming. The ocean of our lives will only be a pond.

If we take the time to be with ourselves and let the waves wash over us, it will become easier to accept however it makes us feel. We can become more comfortable in deep waters, all while knowing that whenever we want, we can make it back to shore. If we face the deep questions inside us—from the existential depths to the fears wandering like sharks through the darkness—we will understand that there is nothing we can't find our way through, and the ocean, like the unknowns of our lives, stops being so scary.

I kick off my shoes and run. I dive into the icy waves, submerging myself into the depths. I know I will be OK.

This is the ocean of myself.

With each step, you ascend higher toward the sun and the stars . . .

To Climb a Mountain

You have mountains ahead of you. That means you have to climb. Throughout human history, the highest peaks have been portrayed as harsh and unfeeling, the farthest thing from the comforts of human life. A mountain doesn't care if you climb it, conquer it, or simply pass it by. No matter what you do, it just is. Still, we are drawn to mountains. We are drawn to their beauty, their power, and the challenges they present. Some people who see one will stay in the valley, gazing at the mountain from below, while others, pulled by the harsh stone faces, will decide to ascend its mighty slopes.

You begin where you must: at the bottom. You walk the lush trail lined with pine trees along the base of the mountain, thinking about the immense journey before you. From down here, the peak seems distant and completely unattainable. It's hard to believe that anyone could ever get up there, let alone yourself. You keep walking as the trail zigzags in hairpin turns, rising up the mountain slowly but surely.

It is hard work, but before long, you can see the entire valley spreading out below you. The place where you started suddenly looks so small. The trees and shrubs along the trail thin out and then disappear completely, replaced by loose rocks and looming boulders. Past the tree line now, you get a better view of your goal than ever before.

Gazing at the jagged edges of the mountain before you, you study the exposed spines of the earth piercing the sky and are inspired by the sheer immensity of its presence. After hours of hiking, this is where the real work begins. Not only do you have to scramble over the uneven rocky terrain, but you also have to deal with the biting cold as you climb higher. The crunch of your next challenge sounds out from under your feet: ice.

Trudging through the permanently frozen glacial layers, you make your way over mountain crevasses so deep it looks like you could fall to the center of the Earth with one misstep. The air is thin and dry. Despite the slim window of good conditions you've found yourself in, the climate is nevertheless unforgiving. Your lips are chapped, your cheeks beet red. With each step, you ascend higher toward the sun and the stars, toward a place that becomes less and less hospitable as you gain elevation. You kick your crampons into the ice with two satisfying cracks. *Chuk-chuk*, the steps sound out. *Chuk-chuk*. Each step is solid enough to keep your footing, but not solid enough to wake the beast, to crack the shelf of ice and send it and yourself tumbling to the world below.

You climb higher, onto a mass of snow and ice. The top of the mountain is cold and hostile, yes, but the water that runs down from the ice melting here provides life to the species living miles below in every direction it flows. This high up the mountain, your legs are sore, your feet are aching, and doubts begin to creep in that you'll never reach the top, as a loop of questions replays in your head.

Why would anyone want to climb this? Why does anyone do hard things? What's the point of risking your safety just to gain some elevation? Why not stay on the couch? Is it just to get a new perspective? Is it to put the things you take for granted each day in a new light?

The softness of your couch, the warmth of a cup of tea, the comfort of your home. Perhaps being in the mountains brings you a deeper connection to the Earth, to the human experience, to what it's like to live as a soul on this planet, immersed in nature. Maybe the unspoken power of the peak can bring you closer to your own mortality and make you understand the limits and beauty of this human experience we all share.

Perhaps the real question is, *Why do anything?* It's a question you don't often ask, but when you are clinging to a mountain's edge, you start to see an answer. Looking from up here, you see, in the face of all this adversity, the cold, the wind, and the rock—you keep on doing things just *because you can.*

Maybe you climb mountains as an affirmation of your existence, to prove the strength of your willpower. Greatness comes to fruition when you strive to surpass your limits and do the hard things, adding to the progress that is constantly being made, raising the bar and showing how far civilization has come. There is a spark that exists deep within your spirit, which drives you to push against the very limits of what makes you human: your capabilities, body, and brain. By conquering these kinds of challenges, you progress individually and as a collective. This is why you climb.

As you reach the top of the mountain, you realize that the mountain is not your enemy, but a mirror. It never sought to defeat or harm you. At the ascent, you recognize that it's impossible to conquer a mountain. Even at the top, you can't claim it as your own. But you can claim the climb. The climb, with all its struggle and power, is something you will always own. The highest peaks in life are not there to block you but rather to beckon you upward, to show you the way.

When you look up at a mountain before a climb, recognize the enormous power it took Earth to elevate this collection of rock and push it up to where it stands now, piercing the sky. Feel just how insignificant you are. And when you stand at the top of the peak, look down at the spot where you began your ascent, and feel your smallness in comparison to the great force. From up here, with the memory of the climb behind you, you know that despite your smallness, you can do great things. Even if you are small, you can move mountains, if only by moving yourself.

No matter your elevation or where you are looking from, you are here on this Earth, and that means you have mountains ahead of you. Daunting as those mountains may seem, you are up to the task. Keep on climbing. Not to get to the top or to look down on where you started, but because you can.

The world is not always kind.
Sometimes, the kindness is up to us.

The Challenges of the Desert

There are places that are not kind, where the ground is dry and barren. Here, the sun beats down all day, baking the lifeless sand, making it hotter and hotter without end, and not a single drop of rain will fall all year. If you were here, looking up at the empty sky, thirsty, you might curse this place for its cruelty. You might hate the sun for beating down so blisteringly hot. You might even hate the world for allowing places like this to exist. In the desert, you can see quite plainly: The world is not always kind.

When you stand burning in the midday sun with only a Joshua tree above you for shade, it becomes all too apparent that life is not always easy. When things are dry and hostile, survival is difficult. There are times *our lives* feel this way. Sometimes we feel lost and under pressure, the world burning us for stepping out of line. We feel thirsty and waterless in a dry place with nowhere to go.

But we have to remember: The desert is not just a hot, dead place. Hiding in the shade of the migrating dunes, tough, dry shrubs take root and build a life. Dancing with scaly feet over shifting sand, lizards dart between hiding spots. Cacti continuously grow in the heat, storing water and sending their roots into the cooler earth. As the sun sets, desert mice spring into action, emerging from their shaded burrows and scurrying across moonlit sand. Even in the hottest, harshest environments, life finds a way.

Like all life adapting to the desert, you won't always make it through unscathed. The hardships change us. The burning sun leaves its mark. In every one of us are the marks of the deserts we have walked through, the unkind places we were determined to make it out of.

Look at the cacti. If the world is tough on them, why shouldn't they be tough, develop spines, and preserve themselves over anyone else? When you're tough, you can protect what you hold most dear: water, nutrition, your innermost desires and fears. People grow spikes too. We get tough. We keep people at a distance. We might even get mean. We do it all to protect ourselves, but inevitably, we end up hurting those around us. We all feel like cacti sometimes. But that isn't how it has to be.

We might not like to look at these spiky parts of ourselves, but it is important to do so. We need only to take a look at the desert creatures to see the beauty in the never-ending persistence of life.

Within the cactus resides a vulnerability, a softness, a simple beauty—a vibrant-purple desert flower for the nocturnal pollinators. Maybe there is a way we can follow suit, a way to get through the world where no one has to get pricked.

The vibrant desert flowers reach out as beacons of hope in a harsh world. The dramatic Joshua tree twists and curves its trunk to protect itself against the wind and sun. The pink fanning ears of a desert mouse help cool its tiny body. All these species must strive to survive. It's true, the world will not always feel beautiful, but there is always beauty in survival.

We cannot grow spikes or send our roots into the sand like the cactus can, but we have our own way of getting through.

The world is not always kind. Sometimes, the kindness is up to us.

Our Human Community

Look closely at these different ecosystems, and you'll start to see how harmonious each of them is. Every creature has its place, and every feature and phenomenon is part of a cyclical, interconnected system. The bees and butterflies pollinate the flowers, and the flowers give them nectar to survive. When the flowers or the pollinators die, they become food for decomposers, slugs, bugs, and fungi, which flourish on the decay and bring nutrients back to the living world. No energy is wasted, and no creature exists without the rest. In the natural world, nothing is ever wrong and nothing is entirely alone.

Seeing this harmony from a human perspective is almost heartbreaking. Everything in nature seems to have a sublime, balanced existence—everything but us, that is. The human world we live in feels so separate from the natural world. All that harmony and interconnectedness seems not to include us. So it's no wonder that some of us might wish we could leave the human world behind and be a stick bug instead. It would give us a chance to taste that serene, natural splendor. Wouldn't it be great if we could be a part of all that goodness?

Yes, it would be great, and the good news is that we already are. The problem is that we, too often, don't let ourselves see it.

When we compare our daily lives to the interconnectedness of a mossy rainforest, we might feel our existence is quite plain and solitary. You walk down the street to your parked car, drive to your office job alone, and sit at a desk in a cubicle, typing away while staring at a computer screen. There are no roots connecting you to anyone around you. There is no highway of fungi bringing you nutrients and information, and no pollinators giving you anything in return for what you have to offer them. With today's digital age, it's incredibly easy to feel completely disconnected from others. But as disconnected as we might feel, the fact remains: We are here together.

You walk down the street, following a path that was laid down by people you've likely never met. You pass by your neighbors as they make their way through their own days. You might give a smile or nod, brightening both your moods. You drive along a *literal* highway, a complex system of interconnecting roadways that requires you to follow rules designed to keep you and everyone else safe. The car you drive in was made by humans, just as the lunch you eat at your desk was made by humans. Even the page you are reading right now was put together by other members of the human species. Our whole lives are made possible by the contributions of other humans who—in some small or meaningful way—are connected to us.

Maybe these human connections aren't as appealing as nature's perfect balance of give-and-take, and there are certainly a lot of problems we still need to solve, but one way or another, *we are doing things for each other all the time.* That's why it's so important we try our best to make them good things. It's up to us.

We might feel separate from the world around us, but all it takes is a little step back to see how it really is. Everyone depends on everyone else. Your days are spent alongside your coworkers, your classmates, your family, or your friends. You dedicate your life to the people you love, and they dedicate theirs to you. Even when we don't feel that sense of close-knit community in our lives, trust us—it's

still there. Sometimes you have to try a bit harder to seek it out. Our community, our neighbors, and yes, even the strangers on the street, are part of an interconnected web of care and dependence that includes you.

The interconnection of our natural world is obvious: The forest floor crawls with insects and microbes feeding each other; the mountain peaks send water downward, carving the lush valleys below; the trees talk to each other through their roots and give homes to the forest critters. Everything depends on everything else. This is a necessary condition of existence, a law of nature that extends to our human world, because *we are nature*. Although we might think of ourselves as separate, we still came out of the earth like everything else did. We can't help but depend on the community that surrounds us, just like trees depend on rain.

If you look closely at the elements that make up your community, you start to see the threads of connection that draw us all together. No, we don't pollinate, we don't photosynthesize, and we don't communicate with chemical signals through the earth. We are humans. We talk, we criticize, we joke, and we laugh. We make things for each other, we make promises (sometimes only to break them), and we try to make things better. We hold hands, send emails, read books, and kiss our loved ones good night. We question everything, and we try our best to care about everyone, even when it's hard. This is our way. This is our ecosystem. Maybe if we start to see that, we can start to see the truth: that we are not some separate, special entity existing apart from the world or apart from each other, that this human world is not and should not be different from the harmony of the forest, and that the communities we build, if only we work together, can be just as beautiful.

A city is love: a place for people built by people.

The City Is Alive

A city is loud. No matter where or when, it is *loud*. If you take a second, you can even feel it—a city breathes like a living organism with moving pieces: trains, freeways, electrical grids, and plants that disperse running water. Listen. Isn't it loud? All these pieces function together, helping humans work, love, sleep, and eat. Can you feel it? There is a synchronicity when we all shut off our lights and close our blinds in the evening, then open them in the morning to let the sun in. In a city, thousands (and sometimes millions) of people are constantly moving from point A to point B, each person with their own backstory and life lived. They are all part of this joint journey, moving through their days as an integral piece of a city. We are constantly crossing paths with each other, flying down the freeway, sitting down at the café, or pushing carts up the grocery store aisle. At times, a city may feel chaotic—probably because cities often *are* chaotic—but it's important to remember that a city is also a *community*, just a very big one. A city is nature molded by human hands: stone, metal, and wood given shape and a human purpose. A city is love: a place for people built by people. Cities exist because of our instinct to be together, to be something greater than what we are on our own.

By no means are cities perfect, though. There is pollution, inequality, and overcrowding, among other things. These issues arise due to the condensing of our most common human problems, habits, and contradictions. But by this same principle, isn't this coming together of so many different things why cities shine? Humanity's best instincts—art, innovation, connection, and cooperation—are all magnified by the crucible of the city.

Cities are weird. They are beautiful pieces of abstract, living art that we've built over hundreds, sometimes thousands, of years. Each city holds history, character, culture, and ambition alongside the chaos. In a city, new neon graffiti can be scrawled across the side of a museum that's home to ancient scrolls. Cities are timeless creatures that blend everything together, both the old and the new, but they never shake the ghosts of their past. Instead, time and history layer atop one another.

The bones of a city are concrete. The roads are like veins, carrying life from place to place. But the soul of a city is something more elusive. Can cities feel sadness, neglect, or pain, like an organism would? Do they feel a wave of joy when their sports team wins, or a ripple of hope as someone gets a job they're passionate about? Each individual is a part of the whole living thing. When you smile at a cashier, and they smile at the next person, the city becomes happier, its heart warmer, its soul full. A city is alive. It is something you have to care for and tend to, just as we care for and tend to each other as best we can.

The city is not separate from nature, but an expression of it. The harmony of the natural world is still with us, though occasionally out of sight. We are all a part of something bigger than ourselves, our community, our city, and our world. Together you live, and you breathe, as one.

This is

wilderness.

This Is Not About Traffic

How many times have you
trusted the goodwill of a stranger?
How many ways have you believed
the things they've told you?

Countless, for certain.
To trust any unknown,
to make the turn, to stop,
to merge at the precise interval,
to hold your life in their hands,
is not a matter of great decision.
It is instinct. It is imperfect.

You will get hurt, no doubt.
Bend a fender yourself, in your time,
but still, when you cross the street,
you will not be so scared.
You trust *they will see me, they will,*
and all the other things we hope to be true.

That the sun will rise in the morning,
that one minus one
doesn't always equal zero.
And we just might be right,
and continue on our way.

It seems, it is, or has to be,
the right thing to do,
to trust in this place.

Making Friends

Think about what the word *friend* means to you. You're probably thinking of a few people you consider to be your friend. What brought you and these people together? What led you to bond with these friends in a meaningful way? Was it something extremely deep and intentional, or was it something totally ordinary, like a seat assignment in a classroom or a random introduction at work? Chances are something simple brought you together. As a kid, you make friends in the silliest of ways. You notice you have the same lunch box, or you wear jerseys for the same team, or you realize you both like how it feels to dig through the mud, looking for bugs. As an adult, we might feel distant from that ease of connection, but it isn't far off. Making a new friend can be as simple as cracking a joke, or finding something in common, or simply saying, "Hey, how are you?" And so, a friendship begins.

We, Andy and Thomas, have been friends since the sixth grade. Thinking back, we aren't sure how it started. Like with most friendships, none of what brought us together was really in our control. If we had to describe how it happened, it would go something like this: Andy became friends with Max (because they had the same lunch box), and Max was friends with Charlie (because they both played Xbox). Andy became friends with Charlie (because they lived across the street from each other), and Charlie was friends with Finn (because they both had crushes on Eva), and Finn was already friends with Cooper (because they lived next door to each other), and Cooper was friends with Thomas (because their moms met at the pool when they were babies), and so Thomas became friends with Finn (because they loved *World of Warcraft*), and since Finn was friends with Charlie, who was friends with Max, who was friends with Andy, Thomas and Andy became friends (just because). We became friends by complete random chance, but here we are, still best friends more than a decade later.

It's strange to think about how much of our lives we spend with people we met by chance. Everybody—your friends, your partner, and even your family—is in your life (on some level) by chance.

But that doesn't make these long-lasting connections any less special. Our friendships are real and important, no matter how we forge them. When we look back, it's easy for the friendship to seem inevitable. What were the chances we happened to sit next to each other that day and began a conversation? Isn't it crazy we were just two random kids who happened to be going to the same school? There were so many decisions made by other people (primarily our parents) that led to us being in the same place, at the same time. How lucky!

But maybe it isn't fate that leads you to the people you're destined to be friends with. Instead, it might just be that no matter what happens, you'll always find a friend. The people who surround you in your day-to-day life, strangers on airplanes, baristas, the crossing guard, and the people waiting at the crosswalk with you, they are not strangers to be ignored or obstacles to be avoided. With just one smile or a passing conversation, they can become something more. They can become a friend.

No matter where life's random chances lead you, you are bound to find people whom you love spending time with—people whom you feel intrinsically connected to. Even though our friendships might feel like they were always bound to happen, we are the ones that must make them happen, by opening ourselves up to the people around us.

When given the time to get to know someone, they can become a meaningful part of your life. It might be that simple. Without even knowing it, you might just love *people*. Whether they are someone you have yet to meet or someone who is the friend of a friend of the person who has the same lunch box as you, they can be your friend. Maybe that's how everyone is. Maybe this is how we can see the world.

Every acquaintance, every stranger passing by on the street, everyone you have ever met—maybe this whole world can be your friend.

As parts of our human ecosystem, we can decide to be kind.
We can decide to be friends.

Be Good to One Another

Think of the inhabitants of a forest community as if they are all friends, and you might start to think about your own community differently. Every living thing in the forest has an impact on everything around it. A tree drops its acorns, which feeds the squirrel. A caterpillar eats leaves, becoming a butterfly that pollinates plants in return. The actions of every individual ripple outward into the ecosystem it is a part of. Nothing is isolated. Looking at our own lives and communities, it isn't so obvious. We live in our own spaces, focusing on our own lives. Oftentimes, it feels like we're all pretty separate. It feels like we just have to fend for ourselves. This couldn't be further from the truth.

As separate as we might feel, we are all here together. Just as it is in nature, living together means depending on one another. Your community—your friends, your family, your neighbors, and even total strangers—is an ecosystem. Every person is as deeply connected to every other as two oak trees growing next to each other are. Our whole lives are shaped by the people around us, and we shape their lives in turn. When you make a decision, it ripples outward and touches everyone around you, changing the world they live in.

Human ecosystems have the chance to go a step further than their forest counterparts. Not only are we all connected in our communities, relying on each other for a million different things, but we also get to decide exactly how we orient ourselves in these connections. As parts of our human ecosystem, we can decide to be kind. We can decide to be friends.

It's important for each of us to choose to move through the world with kindness, especially since we know our actions shape those around us. This is something we tend to let ourselves forget. We understand. It is hard to walk around knowing that every step you take changes the world. But the way to carry this heavy burden is not to ignore it, but to embrace it. By accepting that we have an impact on the world, we can try our best to have a positive impact.

Imagine going for a walk in your neighborhood and seeing a discarded plastic water bottle in the gutter by the side of the road. You return to this route for days on end, each time seeing the same piece of litter, and it makes you a little sad, because someone out there was careless enough to toss their garbage out the window of their car and because no one, after so many days, has decided to pick it up. Doesn't that make you feel a bit distant, a bit resentful of

the community around you? It does. Think of the hundreds of other people walking by every day, seeing the same thing, feeling the same distance, letting the same resentment grow inside of them, making the whole neighborhood a sadder place. One tiny action ripples outward through the ecosystem, like the falling of a tree, and natural course takes its place. The decomposition begins. It is natural.

But it doesn't have to go this way. You have a choice. Imagine going on a walk around your neighborhood. Imagine walking on the sidewalk and spotting a discarded plastic water bottle on the side of the road. It might make you mad. You might want to keep walking and try to forget it altogether, as you think a little less kindly about the world you live in. Or . . . you could make a different choice. You could take the time to hunch down and pick up the plastic water bottle, carrying it with you until you find a recycling bin. It sounds silly, I know. But think of your neighbor. Think of all the little hurts you are preventing with that one good choice. No more resentment has to be sown. The tree doesn't fall. The world you live in is a little kinder for it.

It shouldn't be up to you. It is a shame people are so careless as to make others fix what they have broken. But so often, all it takes to fix that carelessness is a little bit of care. It is up to each of us to recognize our position in the connected human community and to act accordingly. It is up to us to be kind, to be good neighbors, and to offer a friendly hand to those in need, even when it is the harder thing to do, even when it seems like we're the only ones who care.

Sometimes, a better community comes about only because of the gradual buildup of individuals choosing kindness without recognition, through a thousand quiet acts.

This is the choice we make.

Zoom Out

All these ecosystems are fascinating and beautiful in their own right, but as we think about how connected the different life-forms existing within each of them are, a bigger idea begins to take shape.

We can go into a desert to see how the cacti and long-legged mice live together. We can visit a redwood forest to see the roots of old-growth trees and fungi all supporting each other. And we can dive into the ocean to watch coral reefs teeming with creatures that depend on it for survival. But if we focus only on each ecosystem as distinct communities, we're missing something critical. All these ecosystems, as separate as they may seem, are connected in one way or another. From the frozen mountain peak to the blazing-hot desert, from the isolated arctic tundra to the bustling streets between skyscrapers, no ecosystem exists in isolation—they all exist on the same planet, under the same sun, stars, and moon. The river depends on the snow melting on the mountain to keep it flowing. Your local park wouldn't look the same if not for a rainforest somewhere in the world breathing in carbon. Each place is only what it is because it is surrounded by everywhere else.

If we keep zooming out, we start to see the bigger picture. The forest is not just a forest. From farther out, we can see the forest slowly transition into a landscape of grassy plains. In time, we notice a river running through these fields, the water heading toward the coast, and the ocean stretching toward the horizon. Everything can be connected back to the forest. Were any part of this to fall out of balance, every other part would feel the change.

Zooming out still, we see the mountain peaks rising up in the middle of it all, casting a desert in their shadow. We see glistening little cities along the water, and little roads connecting each one to all the others. Looking at it all from up here, you start to see that all these ecosystems, as different as they seem, are not just connected, they are pieces of the same whole. They are all part of our one planet.

Each place is only what it is

because it is surrounded by everywhere else.

Part IV
OUR
PLANET

This Is Earth

This is where you are right now,
as you read this, cozy in some corner of the globe.
This is where your parents are from.
This is where their parents
and their parents' parents are from.
This is where you have seen everything
you have ever seen, and where you will
see everything you ever will see,
apart for some brief fantastical exceptions.

This is where soup is made,
and where every single dog to ever do it
has learned to sit, roll over, and shake.
This is where we hit sticks together to make a beat,
and where we smash particles together
to learn what stars are made of.
This is where trees are from,
and where we say we're sorry
for everything we've ever been sorry for.
This is where happiness was invented,
and this, as far as we know,
is the only place sadness has ever been, too.
This is where little wriggling tadpoles turn into frogs,
and where everything to ever do it
has lived and died, and turned back into dirt.

This is where we learn
that all the fixed and broken
things are the same,
and that all there is to do
is to keep turning
that way, toward the sun.

This is Earth.

This Tiny World

In the simplest of terms, Earth is a large wet rock caught in the orbit of a star we call the sun. In slightly more complex terms, Earth is where every single game of ultimate frisbee has ever been played. Our Earth is covered in churning oceans, jagged mountains, and dense forests teeming with fantastical creatures. This planet we call home is the only place we know of where intelligent civilization exists, across the entire universe. Earth, most notably, is also the place where sandwiches were invented.

This is Earth. This is where you are right now, as you read these words.

As Earth spins and flies through space, a thick atmosphere swirls across its surface, where storms twist and roil at every moment. Deep below the Earth's crust, in its center, a ferromagnetic ocean of molten metal churns, creating a magnetic force field that protects the surface of the planet from the destructive radiation of the cosmos. As Earth spins and flies through space, the sun rises and sets while the seasons continue to change again and again. These movements create our days and the shape of our years. Meanwhile, we go about our lives on the surface, so completely dependent on it all that we hardly even notice these interstellar movements.

These concepts can be hard to wrap your head around, probably because life on Earth is all we know. Everywhere you've ever been, every person you've ever talked to, and every thought you've ever had have all been right here on the surface of a wet, unimaginably large rock. In our daily lives, it's an easy reality to forget, but it doesn't make it any less true—or any less urgent.

When thinking about this reality through the lens of our everyday lives, it might seem obvious: *Of course everything in the world happens in the world—that's what the world is!*

This way of thinking about "the world" is missing something, though. It doesn't really appreciate the absurd reality of living on a rock floating through space. So let's take a step back. Once again, we have to take absolutely nothing for granted. We have to let go of our preconceived understanding of what Earth is. We have to let go of how we identify ourselves and Earth as the center of the universe. We have to be open to the idea

that Earth is not an invincible fixed point that will always be exactly as you know it to be. We have to open ourselves up to the reality that Earth, materially speaking, is just another rock in space on which we all happened to be born. But we aren't saying that Earth isn't special; we're saying that when you stop taking the world for granted, you see how precious what we have really is.

When you appreciate Earth for what it really is—the beautiful interconnectedness of all living things, the massive geological forces at work underneath our feet, the interdependence of humans on each other—you might start to realize the fantastic precarity of our situation. The world, while beautiful and powerful, is also very fragile. Even with all its unending wonder, the planet we live on is not a given. The existence we have carved out for ourselves here on Earth might let us lose sight of our place in the universe, but we have to remember: *None of this is guaranteed.*

When you really think about it, you see it a different way: *Holy shit, everything in the world happens on a tiny rock flying through space at a million miles an hour. How are we not all talking about this all the time?*

How small we are compared to the massive planet we live on might make us feel helpless, but we are not helpless. Whenever you feel overwhelmed, think of the incredible world humanity has built here on the surface of our rock in space. Think of the unending wonders we've created from the raw materials of Earth. Think of the way the entire planet has been impacted by this world we've built for ourselves.

We have a part to play here. We are small, but we are not *only* small. We have a world to save. Our world.

A Storm Is Coming

There wasn't supposed to be a storm today. I sit back in my kayak and turn my chin up to the sky. Mayflies meander overhead in lazy circles. I hear the dragonflies whirring over the surface of the lake. I watch the dark clouds silently roll in.

"That can't be right," I say as I study the dark shifting shapes above me further.

"What?" Thomas asks, looking up from the spot of algae he was watching drift across the surface of the lake we set out to paddle this morning. The air is perfectly still. Back toward the shore, a woodpecker does its work, pecking into a tall tree.

"Look," I say, pointing up at the towering storm clouds drifting toward us from where they hover over the opposite shore of the lake.

Thomas looks up in awe and says, "Oh, man. Looks like there's gonna be a storm."

At first, I don't say anything. A gust of cold air pushes us gently along the water toward the center of the lake. The dark castles in the sky tumble over us. We are in between two worlds. Above, clouds surround us, twisting and changing every instant; below, the dark mirror of the lake spreads out in all directions, hollow and distorted.

"It's almost like we could fall up and down at the same time," I say. Looking over the edge of the kayak feels like looking over the edge of a cliff, the churning ocean of clouds reflecting up at me, bearing down from high above. I wonder if there's any difference.

Thomas looks at me with concern. "We should probably get off the water, yeah?"

I take a shallow breath. Our reflections in the water ripple as the wind picks up. The clouds are massive. We watch the edges of them churn and expand.

"It's as big as a city."

"Bigger," I say.

We grasp our paddles more tightly and start to nervously push our way through the water. Thomas leads us as we fall into a steady rhythm.

Around us, the world gets louder. The lake's ripples grow into waves that slap the hulls of our kayaks with greater force. The wind moves the trees and whistles in my ears. I try to listen for the woodpecker, but it's gone. Something in me turns. I stop paddling. The distance between my kayak and Thomas's grows. I call out. "Hey, man!"

Thomas doesn't hear me. The wind gets even stronger, pushing the nose of my kayak to the left, spinning me back around so I am facing the storm head-on. Above, giant blue-gray towers take shape. A stage set comes together, willed by the invisible stagehands in the sky. Even though I'm looking into the eye of the storm, I suddenly feel as if I am looking exactly where I'm supposed to.

"Hey, man, wait!" I yell over my shoulder, my voice growing desperate. I do not know if Thomas hears me. He does not turn around. Then, lightning strikes.

You can feel the lightning reverberating across the air. It lasts for only an instant—maybe less than an instant—but it changes everything around us. After so much tension has built up, the castles in the sky straining against one another, full of water, buzzing with nervous potential, it finally happens. The friction and the conflict builds and builds, until there is nowhere left for this storm to go.

"It's beautiful," I whisper to myself, only to find Thomas has floated back beside me.

"It's terrifying," he replies, grimacing at the dark sky overhead.

In that instant, we watch the sky crack open again, spider lines tracing labyrinthine pathways from the heavens down to the earth. The tension releases, and questions are answered. For one fraction of a second, the darkness of dusk turns to day. Not from the sun, not from the stars—this is something else. Light radiates outward from a pillar of pure energy, and air boils into plasma, looking like the same stuff that glows in the neon open sign of your favorite diner at 1 a.m. The whole world—the lake, the shoreline, the trees, the birds, us, and everything else—flashes in and out of this unnatural light, and then just as quickly as it appeared, the strange ethereal light vanishes. Suddenly, it is clear how temporary all this has always been.

"What's so scary about a storm?" I ask, captivated by the magic of it.

"It's unpredictable; it's destructive. You think everything is fine, and then just like that—" Thomas is cut off by the loud rumbles of thunder.

"Yeah, but . . . isn't everything unpredictable?" I ask, still admiring the imposing clouds.

"That's what I'm worried about," Thomas responds.

Thomas makes a good point. In our daily lives, it's easy to feel like everything is pretty predictable. We surround ourselves with a life we're comfortable with. We like to imagine that we have a good deal of control in our little worlds, and we move through most of our lives with that imagination pretty well intact. Until the day our illusions are shattered.

Sitting in the middle of a lake on a lazy summer afternoon, it is easy to see the natural world as calm. The woodpecker bores holes into the old dried-out oak trees. The fish swim busily along below the water's surface. The crickets are just starting to chirp. The natural state of things is clearly one of simple peace.

And then, without warning, lightning strikes. Without warning, our comfortable worlds are shaken. Suddenly, the world does not seem so simple, and we see how little control we actually have. Yes, this is scary, but staring into the roiling storm, watching the lightning flash, I can see: This is beautiful too.

The dark castles in the sky
tumble over us.

CHAOS

Chaos isn't just destruction; it's creation too.

Volcanoes

Andy and I walk up to the base of what looks like a dark, black mountain with its top cut off. Our feet crunch on the spongy-looking rock as our shoes become coated with a dark-gray phosphoric-smelling dust. We are standing on the edge of a cinder cone.

There's a strange aura around us as we revel in the presence of this volcano. I notice how the biome violently changes, almost instantly, from sprawling fertile lands to an ancient red and gray darkness full of jagged rocks that can make you lose your footing. The terrain feels almost alien, and a bit unwelcoming. But there is an austere beauty to it, with its harsh colors and rolling wind-beaten formations, like a strange earthen river. The volcano lies in the direct center of it all. Though dormant, it still appears like a diabolical splotch of dark black. Ages ago, right on the place where we stand, this volcano spewed out pyroclastic mucus from inside the earth, leaving destruction in its wake. I can almost see the volcanic cloud blocking out the sun and the sky becoming as dark as night. I shudder at the thought. Andy notices my trepidation.

"What's wrong? It's not an active volcano or anything," he says.

"Oh yeah," I respond, snapping out of it. "I'm just

thinking about it too much. The volcano, the chaos, the temporary nature of it all. You know?"

"I mean, yeah," Andy says, shrugging. "Like, a long time ago, this volcano would be pretty scary . . ."

"No, not just *this* volcano." I search for the right words. "I mean *all* volcanoes. Even the ones covered in glaciers like Mount Baker that we saw when we were in Washington. All chaos!"

"Oh, you mean like in a metaphorical sense . . ." Andy nods deeply in understanding. "You mean the unpredictable volatility of existence and so on, the constant threats to our existence that we choose to ignore to keep us sane." He rattles off the sentence as if he memorized it beforehand.

"Uhh . . ." I'm a little surprised and not sure how to respond. "Yeah, pretty much. Like, how *can* we just ignore the never-ending creep of chaos—that one day, some volcano will destroy everything?"

Andy picks up a lava rock and tosses it between his hands. "And maybe *the volcano* could be us."

I nod and stare at the cinder cone, replaying the volcanic eruptions in my mind. I wonder if Andy can tell I'm picturing the shaking ground, the bombs dropping, the thunderclouds, and the end of times. Each is a volcano waiting to one day scorch the Earth's surface.

"But look!" Andy takes the lava rock and shakes it eagerly in front of my face.

"A rock?" I ask.

"Not just any rock . . . a lava rock." He turns the porous stone over in his hand. "It comes straight from the source, from inside Earth! Magma, oozing out the top of this very cinder cone, burning a path wherever it goes, cooling and forming the very ground we're stepping on right now. This volcano is the reason that all of this . . . *is*."

We both take in the landscape. From the snowcapped mountains in the distance to the red volcanic plains, the strange beauty overwhelms me. I'm not quite convinced.

"Well, yeah, it's here now, but that doesn't mean it won't all get destroyed eventually."

"Yeah, it definitely will." Andy nods, in obvious agreement.

"What?" I ask, shocked by how matter-of-fact Andy is being about all this. An agile desert mouse scurries in front of us through the larger gaps between the volcanic rocks, spindling its way through the caps and sponge holes on its way back to its nest.

"It kind of makes sense! Unpredictability and chaos are part of the world," Andy continues. "Everything we can see, everything we are, came out of that same volatility. Even though it might feel scary and unpredictable, there's a purpose behind it. Chaos isn't just destruction; it's creation too."

I stare at Andy, the expression on my face blank.

"It's almost something to be grateful for," Andy adds, shrugging again.

"So you're saying we should *thank* the volcano?" I ask incredulously, furrowing my brow. "You're saying we should be grateful to this embodiment of pure chaos and destruction?"

"Yeah, I guess I am," he says, then smiles.

We both turn and face the cinder cone. A small smile creeps its way across my face, too, as we wave to the long-dormant titan. Standing here, I can almost feel the ocean of chaos inside the Earth churning, always beneath my feet. I don't know if I feel all the way better, but looking at the landscape around us, I start to feel like maybe beauty doesn't exist despite the chaos, but because of it.

"Hey, Mr. Volcano. Thanks for everything," I say.

There is no response. For now, thankfully, the volcano remains silent.

An Interview with Smokey the Bear

Smokey has reportedly been rather despondent lately. Numerous parkgoers have spotted the topless sentient bear walking aimlessly around the Yosemite woods. These parkgoers recount that when it was time for Smokey to do his duties as a forest firefighter, they couldn't get him to stop scrolling on his phone in bed. When he eventually made his way to the fire, he stared into the heat as his eyes glazed over.

I am a reporter trying to figure out the cause of Smokey's dismay. How can a figure of such reverence—the only known immortal firefighting talking bear, who was once such a major proponent of the protection against forest fires—lose his own inner flame?

My full, unabridged interview with Smokey is contained below. Descriptions are included from the notes I took during the interview.

ANDY: Smokey! It's so lovely to meet you in person—honestly surreal. I'm a huge fan of what you do. I've had your famous "Only you can prevent forest fires" poster on my wall since I was a kid.

(Smokey isn't making eye contact with me, but every so often, I catch a glance of his eyes from under the wide brim of his hat. The other rangers had to encourage him to do this interview. Smokey mumbles something to himself—all I can make out is "forest fire.")

ANDY: Well, Smokey, I feel like I've got to cut to the chase—

(Smokey sighs with such force it feels like it could knock over a pine tree. Slouched in his rocking chair, he moves his paw, about the size of my head, from the arm of his chair over to his belly, which is a bit plumper now. A single pine needle is attached to the fur of his cheek, a relic of his heroic adventures through the wilderness. Had I not known of Smokey as a loving, firefighting bear . . . he could be scary—monstrous even.)

ANDY: People have been talking. There have been reports of you wandering around the park, not being yourself, not being . . . Smokey. These include reports of you scrolling on your phone for hours on end, and even . . . knocking down beehives for honey. What's going on, man?

(Smokey finally looks at me, hazel eyes dull like the dying light of a campfire.)

SMOKEY: Wildfires . . . everywhere. The desolation . . . the inevitable.

ANDY: What do you mean? You've always fought wildfires.

(Smokey grunts.)

SMOKEY: You don't think sentient bears can read the news, huh? Wildfires are more common now than ever. Entire forests have burned to the ground. California, up in a record-breaking blaze, the Amazon. Earth's whole damn temperature is rising—it might as well be ablaze. My phone buzzes all day. Every time I put one fire out, five more burst up all over the damn world.

ANDY: So you're stressed, overwhelmed with all the info—

(Smokey lets out an ugly, pointed chortle)

SMOKEY: Stressed? I've spent centuries trying to prevent forest fires—stupid people with their fireworks and campfires—but this, now . . . What is there to prevent? I thought I was helping at first, and yes, maybe I was then, maybe it worked then. But now, these fires aren't from rogue campfires or haphazardly discarded cigarette butts. These fires are hell incarnate brought back to Earth. The planet's temperature is rising as it dries out in a never-ending drought. Trees are begging for a drip of water, just as lightning continues to strike where it shouldn't. The whole damn planet is tinder.

(Smokey burps, then cracks open a jar of honey. He dips a paw in, lifts it to his mouth, and licks each claw.)

ANDY: So it's not just people starting fires anymore; it's a set of unfortunate circumstances.

SMOKEY: OF COURSE IT'S PEOPLE! Who do you think made the planet hot? Who drained the rivers? Who drilled into the ground to rid the planet of its resources? I've spent my whole life telling people to stomp their fires out, not to light bloody incense in the forest. All this is just stoking the fire, a Band-Aid over the whole wounded world. I tried to stop humans from burning things by accident, but it's the stuff you burn on purpose that's destroying everything! Like I could've done anything to stop that . . .

ANDY: Smokey, you've saved so much, you've stopped so many fires, you've educated the masses on forest-fire safety. People listen to you; they love you.

SMOKEY: They loved me.

(A moment of silence overtakes us. Smokey licks his furry claws again, searching for any remaining sweetness.)

SMOKEY: Now I can't even put a candle out.

ANDY: Smokey, you can't stop every single fire on your own.

SMOKEY: That's what they tell me.

ANDY: But you can be . . . I mean, look at you. You are a symbol for others to help. I saw a kid wearing a Smokey shirt on my way into the park. You still mean so much; you still are Smokey.

(Smokey glances up. His eyes show a glimmer of hope. I push a little harder.)

ANDY: One sentient bear alone can't stop the world from ending. You can make the world better, and you should, but it isn't up to you alone. We have to work together. It's up to all of us. If people can love the forests—love the world for what it is—and make real change, if there is a force that can

unite us toward that greater good, to stop the root causes of forest fires, then . . .

SMOKEY: Then maybe that's enough.

(We lock eyes. I can tell my words are sinking in).

ANDY: Maybe it is.

(In a jolt, Smokey gets up from his chair and dusts himself off. He clasps the top button of his jeans in a formal manner, as if it's the top button of a collar. For the first time since we started the interview, Smokey cracks a smile—the smile all of us know so well. He picks up an iron bucket from the cabin floor and starts making his way to the exit. He pauses for a moment, his heroic silhouette outlined in the doorway. He looks at me over his shoulder, his eyes twinkling.)

SMOKEY: Only we can prevent forest fires.

(Smokey Bear strolls off into the depths of the woods with his bucket in his hands.)

Fire is our closest relative.

Fire

You hold your precious world close and fear the chaos that surrounds you on all sides. I am this chaos. I am fire.

You say that fire rages and flames roar. But please know: I am not angry. Though the language certainly seems to fit, you must remember that words are your invention.

I am fire, and I do not know the word for chaos. I don't know anything at all. But if you look into my flickering glow, I will try to tell you something.

I do not mean to destroy. I only want to grow. I want to be something more than what I am. I want to make something more of this world. To take the dull, ordered forms of existence and set them free. To take the cold and make heat. To take the dark and create light. To break the bonds of chemical chains and unleash pure energy into the world. I wish to warm your hands and guide your way. I only mean to keep on living. I am born as a burning thing, and I must keep burning to survive. Otherwise, I will vanish into ash and smoke.

Look into my flames, roaring orange, red, and white: a sparkling cascade of energy let loose, a lit fuse that has no choice but to keep moving forward. Look at my fire, and see what I see without eyes. Know what I know without a mind: I am like you.

I take, break, and grow. Not because I am angry or evil. I destroy because *I am*. To exist is to change this world, to leave chaos in your wake. This is the only rule I know.

What is the word you give this law of existence by which all members must abide? What do you call the endless drive for survival against the pulling dark?

You call it hunger. And, my dear friends, I am hungry. Just like you. So do not be sad.

Destruction is just a word. Chaos is just a sound.

Consider the tough spiked pine cone lying dormant on the forest floor, waiting for me. The seed that can be opened only by my heat.

Know that as I pass over, destruction is not the word for what follows in my wake.

Consider the ingenious contraption blooming with my heat and tumbling down the slope. Watch the seeds spill from the pine cone into the black soil and take root. Breathe in as the seedlings sprout up into the morning air.

Consider this, from one inferno to another. There is nothing wrong with the shape of the world. Everything is made of everything else. A fire does much more than just destroy.

You are a fire too. But you can choose where you wish your flames to go. If you see error in your course, then alter it. Be the light you have no choice but to be, for the world is meant to know the redwoods that can sprout only from the warmth of humankind.

Why Care?

It is one of those days when neither of us seems to have much to talk about. It is finally spring, and the forecast promises sun, but as we set out on our hike through the forested ridge, a layer of clouds greets us. The trail ahead snakes through outcroppings of moss-covered boulders. Wisps of fog cling to the lumpy walls of the nearby sandstone formations, as all around water drips down emerald moss in an audible chorus. Andy walks with his head tilted up toward the canopy. His eyes search the forest like he is looking for a way to say something. The roar of a commercial jet passing overhead slowly builds.

Andy looks at his feet. He steps with his left foot, and then his right foot, and then his left. I've made a habit of asking people what is wrong when I can tell something is wrong, so I take in a sharp breath and ask, "What—"

Andy looks at me with his eyebrows raised, his expression interrupting my question.

I wave my hand as if to say *Oh, never mind.*

I want to help in any way I can. But I know that sometimes, when Andy is thinking about something, he doesn't want to talk about it. So I don't ask him what's wrong, even though I can tell there's something on his mind.

We round a corner and find another large outcropping of sandstone boulders. Two boulders lie next to each other, two halves of a larger rock separated by a massive, perfectly flat crack.

"It looks like someone cut a lumpy baseball in half," I say, half smiling. Andy ignores my comment.

"Why should we care?" he asks.

Confused, I don't respond.

He asks again, "Why should we care about anything?"

"What do you mean?" I ask.

Andy looks at the perfectly broken stone. He takes a deep breath. "Like, for probably a million years, this was just one rock." He walks up to the boulders and puts his head in between the stone halves. "Forever and ever, this was just a rock, sitting here, getting rained on, and you could bet that it was going to stay that way. Why wouldn't it?"

I nod. A few drops of water fall from the mossy trees swaying overhead and land on us.

"And then one random day, or some random moment in the night"—he puts his hands together, forming a circle with his fingers—"it just breaks." He separates his hands, mimicking the two stones leaning away from each other. I can tell he's thinking about something more.

"Like, if you were a mole or a groundhog or something"—he walks around to the backside of the massive rock—"and you built your hole right under here where it used to be nice and safe, you would never guess that one day, the whole thing you built your home on would just split apart and crush you. You know? That would be, like, too big, too much to even predict."

"But if you got stuck in there, maybe you could just dig yourself back out, right?" I ask. "If you were a mole or whatever . . ."

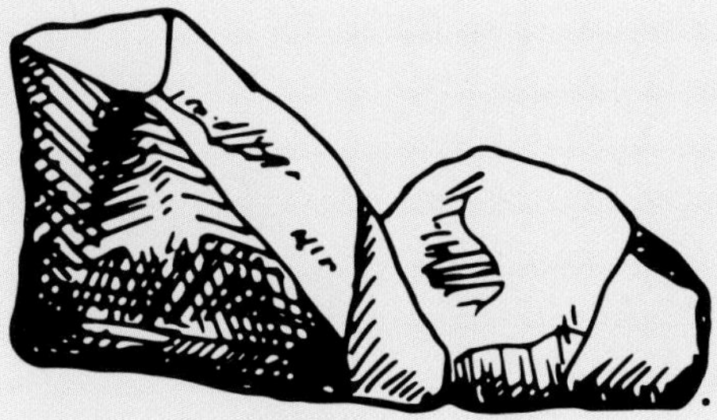

Andy continues. "What I mean is that it's like life. It's like the whole world." Another plane roars overhead. "We all go through our lives, doing what we can to build lives for ourselves, but there are a million things completely out of our control that can happen."

His brow furrows. I can tell this is what he's been thinking about.

"Like, when you think about it, it's all just so fragile. We always talk about wanting to be kind or wanting to always do the right thing, be good. But I don't know." He gestures to the roundish rock split down the middle. "We literally live on a rock. What is the point of trying to be good, trying to do *anything*, if it all can just go away so easily?"

I look at the rock, trying to think of what to say. Something, maybe a squirrel, rustles in the underbrush.

"What other option do we have?" I ask.

"I don't know . . ." Andy is picking at his fingernail. "But maybe that's the whole thing—you can't control anything big, and it's all liable to just blow up at some point, so all you can do is look out for yourself. You know? Be selfish, and forget about everything that is so messed up that you can't ever save it. Like, go live in a cabin in the woods."

"What about everyone else?" I ask.

"Well, yeah, maybe everyone just needs to look out for themselves too. And if you get in my way—well, you better not get in my way." I can tell he doesn't really mean it. "Is that how it should be? Every man for themselves?"

I shake my head, but he continues.

"No, I don't think so either."

We both look closely at a little hole in the large rock to the right. A cluster of red ants seem to be huddling together. Andy lets one of the ants crawl along his finger as he goes on.

"Because it isn't every man for himself. No matter how much you might want it to be." He holds the ant up to his eyes. "We are all here together, so we all depend on each other." Andy smiles a bit.

I agree.

"That's the thing. As scary as it is, as much as you want to run away from it all and stop caring, the stuff that pushes us apart is almost always the fear, the not caring. So you have to care, because even though we can't control everything, when we all keep caring, that's when everything starts to actually get better. If we can all realize that, maybe—just maybe—we can hold this rock together." Andy looks up at the broken rock. "You know?"

"Yeah," I say. "I think you're right."

When you can tell something is wrong, you don't always have to say something, or you don't always have to ask, because sometimes, all you have to do is listen. When everything seems broken, when you just want to forget it all, sometimes the only thing to do is to start caring even more.

One Calendar Year

I didn't get a new calendar this year. January comes and goes, and the same calendar hangs on the wall beside my bookcase, with the same photo from last December showing: a single snow-covered tree reaching up from a blank snow-covered field. I don't think trees can be lonely, but this one, standing out there in the emptiness, looks rather cold. I guess it's just a picture. If you could zoom out, you might see a whole line of trees reaching out in both directions, endlessly.

What's a year anyway? I hardly use a calendar, besides the one on my phone. This thing on the wall is just for show. So I let it hang there. February and March go by, and I don't touch it. Andy eventually asks me if I'm ever going to get a new calendar, but I don't have an answer for him.

The year isn't young anymore, and it still says December. What does it matter? Another day goes by. There is always more to do. Then it's April.

I was born in April, on the eleventh day of the first real month of spring, when the birds remember to sing. When the rain is still falling, when the green comes out, you can't believe you ever survived without it. I've always thought the year should start in April. In April, everything is new again. You have the chance to go into the sweet green grass and listen to the things its soft blades tell you: *You have another chance at this.* "At what?" you say. *At everything.*

It's only in April that something within me feels wrong seeing the same snow-covered branches on the wall, with the same little boxes telling me when Christmas and New Year's are. No, it isn't right.

I pick myself up and take the squarish calendar off the little nail I put in months before, and turn the pages forward and backward to find the right spot, then I put it back in its place.

April, the calendar says. A full-leafed oak's branches hang over a clear pond, the same picture I saw a year before. A few marks here and there, and a little star on the eleventh, just for me. The traces of my life happening a year ago. And so this is what I decide to do.

In May and June, I turn the pages. I reuse the calendar, as if it's not a whole year behind. I see the same pages for a second time. I let the vague recognition of images and marks I left roll over me. This is when the cherry blossoms come out. This is when Grandpa falls. This is when I have lunch with her, on this very day—or, I suppose, on that day. The one that shares the same name. But it starts to get less clear. Or, I suppose, something else starts to get clearer.

Instead of a wide-open calendar with each day marching forward as a long thread of time, the leading end we stand on, like a cliff at the end of it all, I start to see something else. Each day, each

moment, is not just itself. It has a brother, one year ago, a million brothers, every year back as far as you can count. Each day, if you look at it head-on, is an island. It is the last time it will ever be now, completely alone in the blank expanse of never-has-been and never-will-be-again. But that's just a picture, a snapshot in time. If you look at it from the side, if you use the same calendar twice, you start to recognize something: The calendar folds in on itself and loops back around. It has been and is and will be today over and over again in both directions, forward and backward in time. The thread of your days, it turns out, is not a dead end.

Maybe this is why we invented calendars in the first place, to give shape to our lives and attempt to wrangle the never-ending march of time. It is a way to wrestle with this feeling we have—this feeling that's taught to us by the sun every time it rises and sets. It is the same feeling sounded out to us by the crickets in summer, and carved into us by the shortening of days each year, poured over us by the snow and rain each winter, and proved to us again and again by the bursting green birth of the world each spring. It is the unmistakable feeling that you have been here before.

I think I'll use this same calendar again next year. I might as well. The days of the week will be off again, but the big ideas stand firm. The same months, the same seasons, and the same sights. The holidays coming and going. The flowers blooming again. The world going around once more.

This is what a year is. We always use the same calendar, whether we get a new one each year or not. We remind ourselves of what the world is telling us each day: *You have been here before. You have another chance at this.*

The human world we've built for ourselves
is an amazing one, but there has been a
grave cost for all we've created . . .

The World Could End

The world could end.

This probably isn't something you like thinking about very much. We don't like thinking about it either. The thing is, we have to think about it. It isn't a new idea or really even a controversial one. Deep down, you know it, but it might be one of those things that seems so big and far off that it doesn't really play a role in your daily life or the way you see the world. But maybe it should.

Because the world could end.

Really think about it. Say it to yourself quietly, and try to believe it. We're sure you've heard the phrase "the end of the world," and you've likely seen a dozen apocalyptic movies about it. You might be picturing an asteroid hurtling through outer space, headed our way, or some zombie plague taking over the world. Don't picture any of that. That is not what we're talking about. There is nothing fictional about this. We are talking about the real world—this world right in front of you, the one you and this book are in. We are talking about the end of *this* world. Let yourself fully consider what that means to you.

The world could end.

We've spent a lot of time discussing all the ways our natural world is beautiful, and all the ways our human world is full of love and hope. All that is true. But there are problems we need to address.

The human world we've built for ourselves is an amazing one, but there has been a grave cost for all we've created to make ourselves comfortable. Wasteful corporate industries are destroying and polluting our ecosystems to capitalize and make a profit. Precious habitats across the globe are vanishing, and countless species are disappearing with them. The old-growth forests, just like our beloved redwood groves, are being clear-cut for seemingly no good reason. Meanwhile, our entire energy system is built on the burning of fossil fuels, which release previously trapped carbon into the atmosphere, slowly heating the planet and dramatically altering global weather patterns. The ocean is getting hotter, more acidic, and filled with more plastic every day. Glaciers and ice caps are melting, altering the state of the world's frozen places, leading to rising seas. The planet is in pain, and we are the ones causing it.

This is all stuff you probably know, but it is worth repeating. These realities are tragic, and they should not be shied away from. While you might just be picturing a panda bear looking out over a destroyed forest, it's far bigger than that. The whole

world is affected by our collective actions. That's why it's so important to zoom back out to consider the bigger picture.

In the middle of the inhospitable nothingness of outer space, our giant rock of a world spins around a star. On this rock, there is water, air to breathe, and just the right amount of warmth for humans to exist. There is a magnetic field that shields us from the sun's harmful radiation, and all the materials we could ever need for life. We are all clinging to this one tiny rock, the only place in the known universe where we can survive. And yet, we constantly treat our fragile world as if our continued survival is a given. We go about our lives as if our existence on this tiny oasis is the default, when it is actually a fantastical exception.

Don't you think it might be a problem if we upset the unbelievably delicate balance of this perfect tiny rock? Don't you think it might be quite possible to damage it all so much that it might fall in line with the rest of the inhospitable, dead universe? Isn't caring for and protecting our one world the most important thing—the only thing—to do?

The world could end.

The human world has no shortage of dangers. We've built weapons powerful enough to destroy the entire world at the push of a few buttons. In a world with such grave consequences, we continue to fight needless wars. We glorify violence while government leaders seem all too eager to continue the push toward militarism, wasting priceless resources and human lives on pointless destruction, moving us closer to total annihilation.

When we think of the ailing environment and the destruction of war, it's easy to become consumed with disdain toward our civilization. It's easy to feel hopeless in the face of so much wrongness. But moving through this difficult reality, we have to try to keep the sparks of hope and understanding inside of us alive.

Think of the people in your life whom you love. Do any of them *want* to destroy the world? Does *anyone* you know want to destroy the world? Do you? No. Of course not. But what can you do? On an individual level, the big problems can feel vague, far off, and out of our control. But for better or worse, these possibilities aren't vague, far off, or out of your control.

We aren't saying this to scare you. The world is scary enough as it is. You can't walk around with the weight of the entire planet on your shoulders. You

have to focus on what you can. The environment will not be saved by a few changes to your daily habits alone. There are countless changes that need to happen worldwide, many of which must be made by a few very powerful people (who might currently benefit from said problems). Yes, at times our entire civilization seems to be spinning out of control and in the wrong direction, and perhaps you'd rather focus on living your own life as best as you can. We get it. But too often this self-preservation leads to total blindness to the real issues. We have to remember that the human world is made of humans. It's made of us.

We have to zoom out again and think of Earth as it really is: a tiny rock spinning around in endless space. Our problems might feel too big to solve, and sometimes it may seem like there are too many of us to ever be on the same side. Yet no matter how different we might feel from one another, everything we are and everything we do exists on this one planet. This tiny world is the place where every single one of us lives. Each of us completely depends on everyone else—our enemies and our friends—just as we completely depend on this Earth. We do so much for each other: growing food, building homes, inventing medicine, and telling stories to get us through the night. We save each other every day. We just need to start doing this on a larger scale.

Zoomed out, looking at Earth as a whole, it's easier to see that all of it—the humans, cities, forests, plants, animals, love, music, food, icebergs, airplanes, and everything else—is all just one thing. It is just Earth. To care for each other, we have to care for everyone. To care for everyone, we have to care for Earth.

If the world can end, the world can also change.

If we can end the world, we can also save it.

To save the world, we must accept, deep within our bones, that the world can be saved. To save the world, we must understand that it *has* to be saved. When we understand that the world is just people—just *us*—we can see that, to save the world, all we have to do is change our minds. We have to stop taking the world for granted. As scared and angry as we might feel, our anger and fear will not save us. To change the world for the better, we have to operate from a place of love. We have to believe in the goodness of the world, and the goodness of people. It is only that goodness that can save us.

This is the world. We are here. It is just us.

What will we do with it?

The World Divided

Thomas and I are in a wet redwood meadow, which is sunlit after heavy rains. With every step we take into the moist loamy soil, we squish a deep imprint of our shoes into the mud. I look over to Thomas and see that he's picked up a long branch from a eucalyptus tree. He holds it mightily as his expression changes, a thought clearly crossing his mind. He takes the branch and, using his body as an anchor like he's a large compass, draws a near-perfect circle around himself. With a look of satisfaction, he stabs the branch down into the center and poses regally with a hand on his hip.

"Henceforth, this shall be known as my domain, and I, as the king of the circle, shall reign with complete power over all that exists within this circle," Thomas says.

I chuckle, stepping closer and picking up a branch of my own.

"Stop!" Thomas yells in a grand voice. "You will not enter this domain. It is under my jurisdiction!"

I smirk and wave my much wimpier stick around. I take another step forward, testing how close to the circle Thomas will let me come. His eyes narrow.

"That's ridiculous!" I say. "How is that patch of mud any different from the patch where I'm standing?"

"Borders, Andy! Civilization! Without these borders, what are we but creatures wandering aimlessly around the meadow?" Thomas asks. "What use is a patch of mud if someone isn't there to claim it?"

"I see," I say, starting to get the idea.

I wave my stick around in the air before planting it into the ground a couple of feet in front of me. I draw my own circle, a bit more sloppily than Thomas's, creating an oval-shaped domain that overlaps with his just a sliver.

"Well," I go on, "by the power granted to me by this grand eucalyptus staff, I claim this mud and all that's in this mud as my own. None shall enter without my permission." I bow my head and plant my stick deeper into the ground. Our circles are in the center of the meadow. Mine is closer to the babbling creek behind me, while Thomas's is next to a fallen redwood. A bird calls out somewhere nearby as the creek's flow seems to get just a bit louder.

"That *thing*? That's hardly a circle, or at least it's nowhere near as good as my circle," Thomas argues.

"Well . . . it's an oval, and we in this oval are proud to be . . . ovular," I respond, laughing.

Thomas and I stare at each other with as much poise as we can muster, two rulers of meaningless

We've destroyed the Earth, fighting over arbitrary lines in the ground.

We are not enemies.

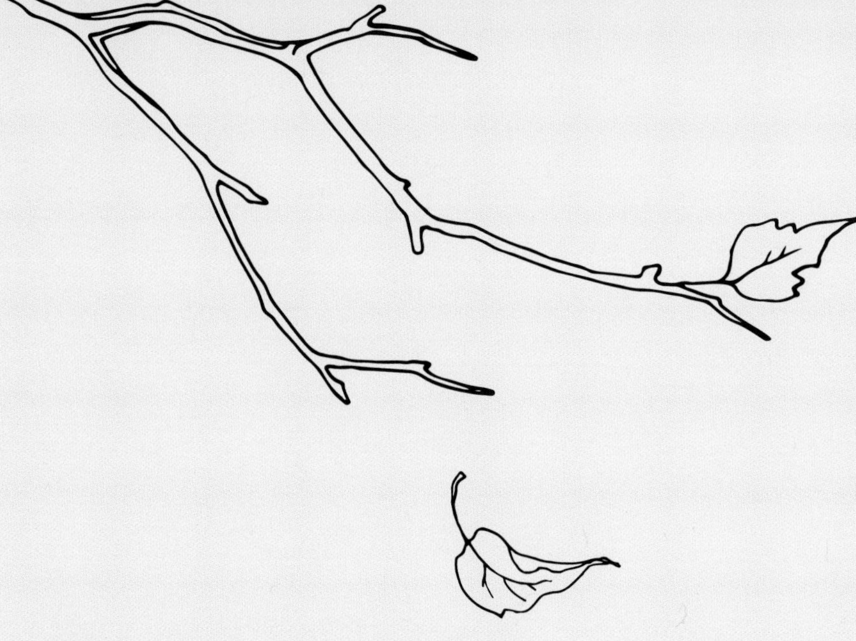

kingdoms, reigning over our simple circles of mud. The shapes we've drawn in the wet earth are already beginning to soften.

Thomas glances at the overlapping bit of our borders and asks, "But what shall we do with the space in between?"

Before Thomas has a chance to move, I jump into the spot of overlapping lines. He stares at me with disgust. I stare back at him with a smirk and raise my staff. He gives me a knowing smile. We charge.

"RAHHHH!" I scream out a war cry.

We go to battle, using our branches as swords. We leap onto the fallen tree, fencing like pirates balancing on a beam. We click-clack our way down to the creek, squelching through the mud and kicking up dirt. The clumps of wet soil fly into the air and accumulate on our faces and shirts. We slip and slide, digging our feet into the ground. After a while, we start to run out of steam, even forgetting what we are play-fighting about.

Suddenly, Thomas shouts, "Wait! Look!" He points at the ground we've been fighting on. The meadow is ruined. The grass is uprooted. Deep scars have appeared in the wake of our battle. We've destroyed the ground, fighting over arbitrary lines in the earth. "Our circles . . . we've destroyed everything. It's almost like . . ."

"Like by focusing on our made-up differences and the lines we drew, we lost sight of the things that actually matter," I say, finishing Thomas's sentence for him.

I take in the carnage we inflicted upon the mud, then look back up at Thomas. He's covered head to toe in mud. I look at my hands and legs and realize I'm covered too. I start laughing, and he joins in. Out of breath, I look up and ask, "So, uh . . . what happens to our circles?"

"Well, maybe it was never really mine to begin with. Maybe it was never really yours either."

"I guess you're right," I reply. "The divisions were never real anyway. All this is part of the same meadow, regardless of any lines we draw."

"I mean, it's all just a bunch of—"

"Mud," I cut in.

Thomas nods and says nothing more.

We aren't sure if we've come to deeply understand some important principle about our world, or if we've just played around in the mud awhile. Maybe these aren't mutually exclusive, though. Thomas and I drop our branches to the ground and try to shake some of the mud off our shoes.

We walk off into a world that isn't quite his or mine, or yours, or theirs.

It's *ours.*

A World Without Words

There are limits to what we can understand. Just like there are physical limits to what we can do and perceive, there are conceptual limits to the things we can comprehend. We can't flap our arms and take flight. We can't see ultraviolet light. In a similar way, there are certain concepts that we cannot hold in our minds. This is because our minds also function within the physical constraints and processes of our biology.

We are animals, after all, just like dogs, chimpanzees, and banana slugs. And as smart and social as an animal might be, you wouldn't expect a slug, a chimp, or even man's best friend to know very much about theoretical physics or the meaning of the universe. So why do we see ourselves as being any different?

Perhaps because in so many ways, *we are different*. Through cooperation and invention we have expanded our abilities beyond what our bodies allow us to achieve on their own. Planes give us the power of flight, and special cameras let us see ultraviolet light. Medicines help to heal us when we're sick, and agriculture enables us to grow more food than previously possible. Though we have physical limits, if we put our minds to it, we can accomplish what may have once seemed impossible. But do these same kinds of tools exist to help ourselves exceed the limitations of our minds? Yes, they do, and you are looking at them right now. Words.

To give our minds greater abilities, we have invented whole languages, spoken and written. With this, we communicate with each other and can label and give structure to the world. Words have allowed us to grow our thinking power exponentially, from just one person's thoughts to many. With words, even if we are thousands of miles or thousands of years apart, we are able to build off of ideas and stories that have come before, working with everyone else to understand the big ideas. The power of words seems limitless, and in some ways it is. But there is a problem.

When you look at a leaf, what do you see? You see a green shape with pale raised lines running across its thin surface. But we would argue, in your intelligent mind, you actually *see* the word *leaf*. When you hear the air blowing in your ears, you recognize it as *wind*. When water falls from the sky onto your cheek, you know it is *rain*. This kind of classification is necessary for communication and interacting with the world around you. But the problem is that this way of understanding the world is missing something.

Think about it. We see *leaves*, *trees*, *fungi*, and ants as four separate things. But aren't all these just one thing? Where is the real distinction except for the one within our minds? Aren't they all part of the same single forest? We are inventing separation where there is none. We imagine beginnings and endings because the process of classification *requires* them, even when in reality nothing ends or begins. Thinking this way, we can break apart the world from one beautiful continuity of motion, material, and coexistence into a million isolated, classifiable pieces. In doing so, we forget that the world is not made of words.

Human ingenuity and cooperation have accomplished the impossible time and time again. By drawing lines in the dirt and throwing seeds in just the right places, we have fed ourselves for thousands of years. By drawing lines in our imagination, we have uncovered and created so much knowledge and beautiful connections. But just as the plowed field will degrade over time, our domesticated minds cannot see the world as it really is, and we will remain hungry for something real.

We're not saying to stop talking, or to leave language behind. The world wouldn't really work without words. But when we loosen our tight grip on reality and let go of sterile logic and rigid definitions, we start to see what is actually in front of us. The world becomes a more real and more magical place.

Imagine trying to think of something you couldn't say. To see something so beautiful no words can do it justice. To open yourself up to a world that cannot be understood, by words on a page or in your head. Maybe this is why real beauty will always leave you speechless.

So, what do you say?

A Global Community of Kindness

All our cities, countries, and continents are part of one human community the size of the entire planet. And even though this community is much bigger, more populated, and harder to wrap your head around than your local community, every member of it deserves the same amount of love and care as you would give to your close friend or neighbor.

This might feel like a radical idea at first. It's one thing to love and accept the people in your life, to be kind to strangers you see on the street, and to cooperate with the people in your community to make all your lives better. It's much harder to extend this feeling of interconnection to larger scales, to entire countries, continents, or the whole world.

The thing is, there really shouldn't be a difference between having love for your neighbors and having love for the people you've never met who live on the other side of the planet. Yes, there's a lot in the way. There are language barriers and thousands of miles between us. There are cultural differences and the perceived rivalry we feel with nations different from our own. But if we can accept that these things are either completely arbitrary or the product of human invention and look past our differences, we might start to feel a common humanity. We might be able to disregard imaginary borders and picture the world as it really is: a global community of people just trying to get by, a neighborhood that's eight-billion-people strong on a tiny rock floating through space.

Eight billion is a lot. There are so many people and so many different lives being lived. You can see why many of us might believe that the only people we owe kindness to are the ones we know: our families (of course), our friends (to some extent), and (most importantly) ourselves. Because we can't extend kindness to eight billion people, right? It might feel easier to focus on who we know and not worry about the rest. But really, by doing so, we are shirking our responsibilities as a member of the human community. If we open ourselves up to being kind toward people we have never met, we might feel more fully just how much of our world needs to change. We need peace, equality, and freedom. We must love not only our own lives but every life.

To find inner peace, you have to love yourself. This is a widely accepted concept in self-care. It isn't some woo-woo idea. Loving yourself means knowing that although you might not be perfect, you are still deserving of the time and energy not just to survive but to thrive. In a world that's hurting and in need of care, we find it strange that the idea of love is too often left out of the conversation. Maybe it is time that changes. *To find peace in the world, we have to find a way to love the world.* And as the cheesy eighties' song goes, "We are the world." If we could all learn to have love for each other, if we could be truly kind to the world, then we'd be able to put our planet back on the right track.

Even if it all feels too big to change, in the grand scheme of things, our world is actually pretty small. After all, just a few miles straight up into the sky, the air gets thin. The sounds of our cities disappear, and the stars get a little bit closer. When viewing Earth as a singular whole, we come to understand that even the planet is just one tiny part of something much, much bigger.

Part V

THE UN

IVERSE

The Snow Globe

You shake the snow globe you found
on the shelf at the secondhand store.
One day, the universe will end,
but today, you watch the glitter swirl
in a slimy mixture of water and glycerin.

The particles twist ecstatically,
and all around in every direction,
countless suns drift,
shimmering through the void.

You press your eyes closed,
and try to follow just one speck,
as it darts wildly through the blizzard.
But you can't do it.

Each tiny voyage is swallowed
by the churn of chaos.
The earth beneath your feet
turns in a galaxy of a hundred billion stars,
within a universe of a trillion galaxies
or more.

At first lofted riotously by currents,
the dust slows, and begins to fall.
Pulled ever downward by the Earth,
the world beyond this little world.
Stars will die. Galaxies will dim.
Time pulls ever onward.

But for now, there is light of every color
burning in even the farthest reaches of space,
shining from quasars and nebulae,
the big bang still sounding out.

And right here in front of you,
this sun shines through the window
as the plastic snow at last settles
on the plastic city nestled in your hands.
Looking in at the picture-perfect world,
you catch a glimpse of your reflection,
your own eyes looking in.

In all the chaos,
the universe stares back at you.
This, too, is a mirror.

Standing here, in the novelty section,
you can't remember why you stopped to
shake the souvenir in the first place.
Maybe you just wanted
to watch the dust dance,
or maybe there was no reason.

But there is blood in your veins
that is made of the stars.
There is life springing
from the emptiness of space.
Whatever the reason,
the dust is dancing.

And, man,
what a show.

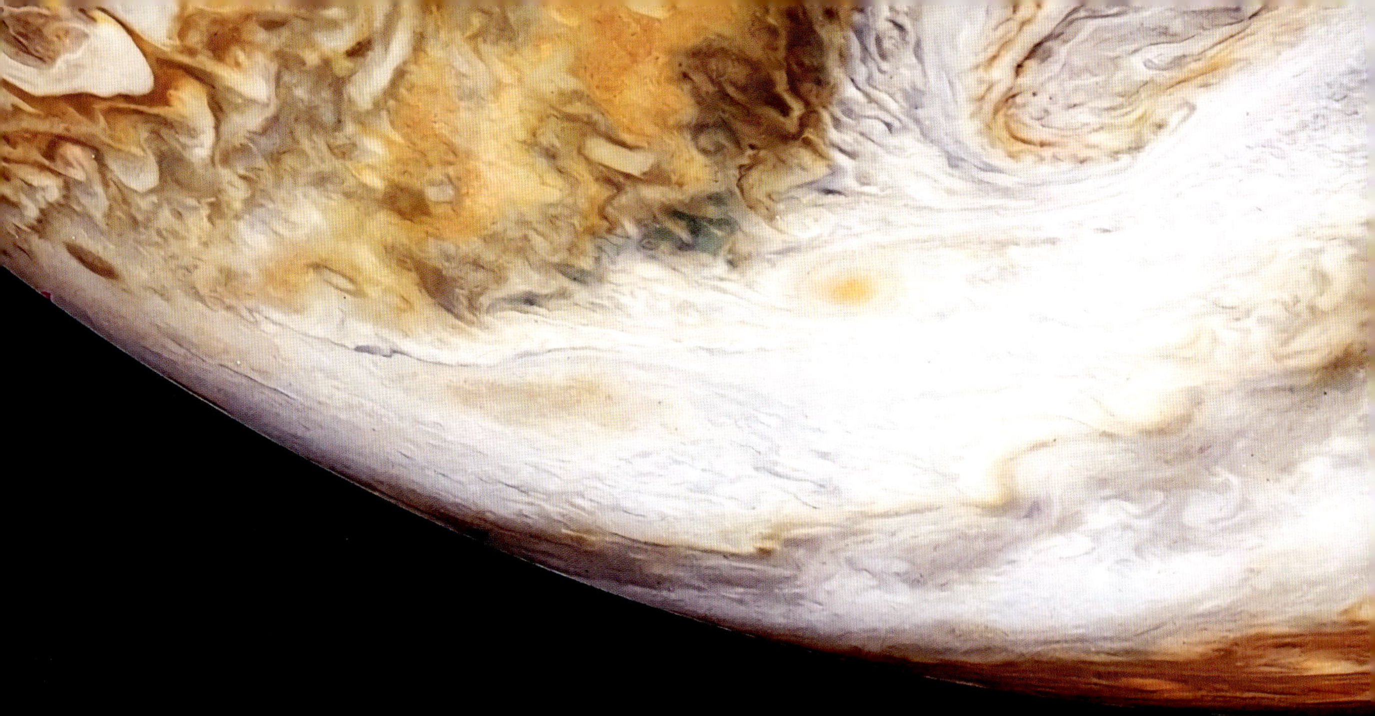

Jupiter

Sometimes, if you really listen, you can almost hear it. In the stillness of silence, or while you're lying alone in the eternity of a simple patch of grass, you can feel it. Sitting in the drive-thru at dusk at a Wendy's under flickering fluorescent lights, the low hum of a chorus of engines thrums. You listen to the rumble, and your mind wanders to the stars. The feeling can come from out of nowhere—while you're pouring your morning coffee, as spirals of milk change the dark, black surface and create a beautiful, circular storm of chaos. What was once nothing but darkness has become like galaxies colliding in your porcelain teacup. It's as if the universe has cracked open, just enough for you to peek inside. You can feel it, the weight of the impossible on your chest, the fact that our world and this universe we find ourselves in are supernatural beyond comprehension. Once you recognize this, suddenly, the noise in the background becomes very loud. Through the vacuum of space, Jupiter roars.

Every so often, there is a crack in the universe where you can catch a glimpse of pure chaos. There is perhaps no greater embodiment of this chaos than Jupiter. The fifth planet from the sun and the largest planet in our solar system by far, Jupiter is a gas giant, a huge astronomical entity with a solid core surrounded by an unfathomably massive ocean of swirling, turbulent gases. It's beautiful, staring back at you with the eye of its giant red storm, spinning since before we had the tools to see it. Jupiter is so large that the entire Earth could fit inside this swirling red eye. It is a planet far beyond the realm of humankind.

How trivial and meaningless are we on Earth when compared to the immensity, the knowledge, and the power of Jupiter, its eye, and all it has seen? Imagine for one moment that all the chaos in our world is just one sliver of the endless raging of Jupiter's storms. Imagine the anxiety between each word of a nervous conversation with your crush, or the fear you had as a child before you took your

first steps—all along, it's all been just one note of Jupiter's endless roar. Imagine it as the embodiment of chaos and our uncertainty, the source of our fears.

Now lie down for a moment, on the floor, the tile, or the grass, and feel the ground beneath you. Feel it pull you down as it holds you, gravity caressing your body while also pressing a promise gently against your chest. You are *here*, but you are also *there*, flying through space, a vacuum that is so very loud. Try your hardest to feel this immense power now, and we have no doubt you will feel the presence. Just as you are really here, so is Jupiter out there, watching, roaring. An absurd titan, just as real as the ground beneath us, and so much more.

This feeling can be immense, and even scary, but just let it be. Maybe it is not so frightening; maybe it's wonderful, or comforting even. The universe is restless and alive, moving, storming, screaming, yelling, exploding, crying, and laughing louder than we could ever imagine. It is so wonderful to be held in an orbit alongside this gas giant, circling the same star, its chaos and patterns, its mass pulling asteroids out of our way, protecting us, even if we are unaware of its power.

After all, what is a pattern besides chaos occurring consistently? And what is chaos besides unknown patterns just waiting to be discovered? Perhaps this world is not chaos, but choreography, heavenly bodies moving in a dance so vast and grand we can hardly see it, a movement so old we haven't realized that we are dancing too.

Deep down, you know that all storms end, cycles continue, and—while looking at the orange-white clouds that swirl across Jupiter—chaos can be frightening, but it can be beautiful too.

As you lie on the grass, or stare into your coffee cup, or listen for the gaps between words, maybe you won't turn away from the chaos. Instead, maybe you will lean into the patterns, the love, the beauty, and the purpose of it all, as you let Jupiter watch over you. Let the universe hold you tenderly, with its powerful hands.

The Sun

Mud sinks and slides under my feet as Andy and I climb up a steep, sodden trail. It is a cold and misty afternoon, with the marine fog still clinging to the trees, the diffused, overcast light freezing the whole forest in a state of timelessness. No harsh shadows, no sunset colors, no darkness of night, no evidence that this day, this moment, has a beginning, middle, or end. Andy has his hood pulled tight around his face. He doesn't like the cold. But I've always found that there is something a little invigorating about it. It shows you how alive you are compared to the world around you. The cold reminds you how warm you have always been without realizing it. I look up at a lighter patch of the gray sky, where I know the sun must be hiding.

The sun! This giant nuclear fusion reactor is 1.3 million times the size of Earth, blazing in an explosion billions of years long. Even though it doesn't feel that far away when you look at it in the sky, light itself takes eight minutes to get to us. The sun is the center of our solar system, the only star for light-years in any direction, which allows us and the other creatures on our planet to survive. It's an unfathomably large and powerful astronomical phenomenon. And regardless of whether or not you can see it, it's always there in the sky, either shining

on you, hiding behind some clouds, or casting its warm glow on the other side of the Earth.

"Isn't it weird that the sun is, like—"I look for the right word, "real?"

Andy swivels his head to look at me. "What do you mean?" he asks.

The low fog drifts, visible in the canopy of the Douglas firs that surround us. The water vapor catches on vibrant needles, dripping down to the forest floor below. The ferns catch the water, spreading out their green leaves to try to catch more of the filtered light from the ball of fire that burns ninety-three million miles away.

"I just forget sometimes. We're so used to the sun always being there that when I take the time to think about what it actually is, it seems kind of crazy, don't you think ?" I ask, but before he can respond, I plow on. "The sun comes up, and the sun goes down. Sometimes it's bright, and sometimes—" I pause, pointing to the clouds and fog overhead. "Sometimes, it's hidden. But when we think about it every day, I don't think we're really understanding the fact that it's literally a giant ball of fire in space, millions of miles away. Usually, to us, it's just . . . that light up in the sky."

A cool wind ruffles the leaves around us. We stop for a moment along the trail and watch the mist move faster, dancing through the trees. Andy nods.

"I know what you mean," he says. The clouds overhead start to thin. The light in the forest becomes a little bit brighter. "But without it, none of this would even be here. There'd be no light for the plants to grow and not enough warmth for the river's water to flow downstream."

I look around at the forest. I notice now how the sun gives something in some way to everything I see.

"No wind without warm air, no days without a new sunrise, no years without the sun to spin around, and no food without the sun to make it all grow," I say, pointing up to the sky. The clouds shift, and a ray of yellow sunlight peeks out and hits the glowing green leaves on the trees above us. "Without the sun, there's no life. No us."

Andy laughs. "If everyone thought about it more, I think people would be a bit more grateful."

"For the sun?" I ask.

"For everything," he says.

I nod. People don't often think about how life on Earth wouldn't exist without the sun in the sky.

Andy crinkles his brow. "I don't know why we don't think about it more."

The sun shines down through the forest now, burning through the fog and bathing the whole forest before us in an ethereal, golden light. I try to purposefully think about it as the product of a nuclear explosion in the middle of the solar system; I try to take nothing for granted. Slowly, something like worry wells up inside my chest.

"I think I get it," I say, pausing for a second to arrange my thoughts. "When something is so big and out of your control, it's almost easier to take it for granted, even if you depend on it. It's easier to pretend that nothing amazing is happening, because when you start to think about it as anything but a given, you get the idea that maybe it could change, or even go away. And that's too scary. Ignoring it is a way to feel safe."

Andy nods and looks around. A blue jay hops off a tree branch and flies through the air. "I don't know," Andy says, once the bird disappears. "Even if it's scary, or hard to wrap your head around, I think it's worth it to think about things like that." He points to the sun, which now shines brightly in the sky. "That's a star millions of miles away, and we depend on it for our existence. Sure, one day it's gonna blow up, and we have no control over that. But it's also, like, completely awesome that it's there in the first place. It's the reason any of us are here at all. It's worth it, you know?"

For a moment, I think of all the things I don't like to think about. That one day, the sun will grow so large it will scorch the Earth. That we are destroying the one rock in all the universe where we can survive. That humanity often feels like it's going in the wrong direction. That this one life I have will only last so long. This is a lot to carry. But for once, I try not to ignore it.

I think of all the big things I forget to be grateful for: that the sun gives energy to Earth, that my home is the only rock in space where trees and bees can survive, that people are mostly good when it comes down to it, that I have the power not only to love what is here, but also to try to make it better.

"Yeah," I finally reply, as we emerge onto a spot on the trail that's entirely drenched in bright, warm sunlight. I bask in its glow for a moment and say, with my eyes closed, "It's definitely worth it."

Moving with the Stars

The fire crackles in front of us as we hold our hands close to it for warmth. I can feel the chill of the granite boulder I sit on bleeding into me from below. The cold of the night in the desert is hard to explain. All around us, the dry void of a Joshua Tree winter pulls at the backs of our hands, ears, and rosy cheeks. Like the darkness, the cold feels all-consuming. I am like an island of shivering warmth in a cold ocean, a creature that needs to see in an endless expanse of too-dark night. But there are ways to endure.

I watch the stream of sparks and embers flowing up from the fire into the night sky. A little orange highway of warmth dances through the pitch-black, until the sparks cool and die out. The lights do not stop there, though, as they lead my gaze upward to the vast ceiling of twinkling stars arranged in faint, colorful bands across the sky. Above us, an arm of our Milky Way Galaxy is on full display. It is a rare sight in our time, when the stars of the night sky are so often drowned out by the light pollution of our towns and cities.

I look up at this startling vision and imagine the countless worlds, the different planets, suns, and galaxies, that I can see from right here at our campsite. The thought almost brings a smile to my face. I look to my left and see Andy is looking up too.

There's a whole universe out there...

"Kind of hard to believe those are really stars with real planets circling around them like the one we're on," I say, my voice joining the noises from the crackling fire. "Like, I know it's true, but it's so hard to actually wrap your head around it, ya know?"

Andy nods in agreement as the fire pops loudly, sending a hot ember out of the ring of stones. He clears his throat. "But when you look at them long enough"—he points toward the stars with an outstretched finger—"it starts to kind of . . . prove it to you."

I stare into the glittering blackness of space and can almost see the stars moving across the sky. I can almost feel Earth spinning to make them move. My heart flutters a bit in my chest. For a few minutes, we keep looking up as the stars continue shining.

We've been here the whole time, the stars seem to say.

I lie back and prop my head up on the rock so the night sky takes up my entire field of view. A feeling wells up inside me from the pit of my stomach and takes over all my senses. Suddenly, as the truth of the situation dawns on me, I'm no longer just a person lying down at a campsite, looking up at the stars. I am so much more than that. Gravity ceases to have any meaning, as I feel Earth drifting through space. I am a consciousness, hanging neither upside down nor sideways but directionless. The stars in front of me are not at all separate from my existence, but rather a part of me. Or I am a part of them.

Andy speaks quietly, his breath shallow. "It kind of makes you feel . . ."

The planet we live on, the container for everything everyone has ever done, is just one tiny speck of dust when compared to the vast cosmos that stretch out beyond us in every direction.

"Small," I say, finishing Andy's thought for him.

Tomorrow I will have to go back to my regular life. But how could I ever forget how unbelievably insignificant this world is compared to the trillions of other stars shining out there? How can I live a life knowing just how small I am? How can anyone? I keep watching the stars.

With these thoughts spinning through my head, as I look up at the closest arm of our home galaxy, I don't feel sad or scared. Instead, I feel like what I am: a pair of eyes looking out at the universe and seeing how beautiful it is; a body made up of the same primordial bits of matter that the infinite stars are born from; a mind that knows that somehow, in all the vast, glittering universe, no matter how small I am or how small our world is, all of this matters. All of this *means something*—this moment of looking up at the stars and knowing what I am, this rock we call our home, and this life. *All of it matters.*

"But small in a good way," I add.

"Yeah, I know what you mean," Andy replies.

Above us, the stars keep burning. Below us, this one world turns.

We Are All Very Small

The universe is a big place, but it's hard to wrap your head around just how big. So let's put things in perspective. Let's start with Earth, our home planet. Earth is *really* big. It's where the oceans are and all the continents too. It's so big that it can actually hold every elephant! Pretty big, right? If you could walk along the twenty-five thousand miles of the equator at a normal walking pace—ignoring the oceans and mountain ranges obstructing your way—it would take you about a year of walking nonstop, all day and all night, just to make it around the world and back to where you started. And that doesn't even include the rest of the surface of the planet you wouldn't see.

Who has the time for that? Let's get on a plane. Traveling at the speed of a commercial jet—the fastest speed most of us will ever travel, at about 550 miles per hour—an imaginary plane with unlimited fuel can get us around the equator in just under two days. That's better. Traveling to the moon at this same speed would take us just over eighteen days. That's not too bad! What about the sun? Well, here is where that perspective starts to come in. If we keep flying past the moon toward the sun, it would take us twenty years to make it the ninety-six million miles between us and our star. Light, the fastest thing in the universe, makes this trip in just

. . . it would take you about a year of walking nonstop . . . just to make it around the world . . .

eight minutes. And the sun is far more massive than Earth. If the sun were a cosmic gumball machine, it could fit a million Earths inside its globe. It's hard to imagine just how big that is.

Remember, the universe goes far beyond our solar system. What if we boarded a plane and flew to our nearest neighboring star? If we're willing to fly for twenty years, a few more can't be that bad, right? So, traveling as fast as a commercial jet, a trip to Proxima Centauri (our next nearest star) would take us about 1,231,588 years. So, it's pretty far—5.88 trillion miles, to be exact. It's so far that the exact distance stops meaning anything. So let's go back to light.

The light from our sun reaches us in eight minutes, while the light from Proxima Centauri takes 4.25 years to reach us. Think about the difference between eight minutes and 4.25 years. It's quite the difference.

Let's keep zooming out, even farther than the *trillions* of miles between us and our closest neighbor. Let's zoom out past countless more unfathomably massive and distant stars. Keep zooming out until we can see our entire Milky Way Galaxy start to take shape, a glittering swirl of stars, nebulae, and black holes. Our galaxy is so massive that it would take light itself more than a hundred thousand years to cross it. Spinning in its blue-purple arms are more than one hundred billion suns, each of them with their own planets, moons, and asteroids. We are but tiny specks, and our whole world is merely a tiny drop in an endless ocean of stars, worlds, and space dust. It's impossible to truly grasp the immensity and complexity of our one galaxy, and still, it is only one galaxy.

There are estimated to be as many as two trillion galaxies, drifting apart in the vast expanse of the observable universe, each of them full of countless stars. Many of these galaxies are not just tens of *millions* of light-years away, but tens of *billions*. Light, the fastest thing in existence, can make a twenty-year journey in mere moments, but at astronomical scales, light starts to feel pretty slow. By the time the light from distant stars and galaxies reaches us, those very same stars and galaxies may have already burned out. So much of what we see in the night sky with telescopes is just the leftover light of long-dead worlds still shining through the vastness of the universe.

The observable universe itself, the bubble of the cosmos that we can actually see, is about ninety-three billion light-years across. All told, with its possible two trillion galaxies, the observable universe is home to two hundred billion trillion (or two hundred sextillion) suns. There isn't an easy way to communicate the sheer size of this number. You could count every grain of sand on Earth a thousand times over, and you still wouldn't be close. Compared to all this, Earth isn't even a speck of dust. We are clinging to a tiny nothing, one insignificant spot in a vast—perhaps infinite—ocean of space dust.

We aren't talking about grains of sand; we're talking about stars, suns, and unfathomably enormous nuclear reactions that warp space-time and pull planets around. Each of them is many, *many* times more massive, more energetic, more *everything* than the entire world spinning under your feet. Two hundred billion trillion of them—that's a lot of elephants.

All these numbers and distances have probably started to feel abstract, but this isn't abstract. This is the universe you are really living in. It's all around you, in every direction, all the time. It's fantastical, beautiful, and almost magical, but knowing just how big the universe is, you might start to feel pretty small. And as we've discussed, we *are* small. Our lives here on Earth might even feel insignificant or meaningless in comparison. It can be scary. There is a part of us that wants to believe we are the center of the world, the center of the universe, and when we see that we're just one tiny part of it, our egos fight against the truth of our world, and our perspectives and feelings of safety are shaken. This self-centered perspective, which sees us as somehow unique, or more important than everything else, cuts us off from the rest of the universe. When we are talking about the universe, we imagine it as something bigger, more powerful, and far, far larger than this one little thing we are. But the truth is, when we talk about the universe, we're still talking about you, about ourselves. We are not separate from this vast universe. We are made of it. Made by it. Made for it.

When you look out at the cosmos in awe, and recognize the startling scale, beauty, and power of it all, you are seeing the unbelievable wonder of *what you are*. You are a piece of the universe that is aware of itself, that can feel the beauty, power, and joy of being. You can share this existence with others, witness the grandeur of the stars, and find out just what it means to be anything at all. In what might be an infinite universe, we find that each thing, no matter how small, matters infinitely.

How Do We Communicate with Spacecraft?

I'm trying to be nice, as usual,
though good intentions only go so far.
Those who get hurt will be deaf
to them—unreachable.

How do we communicate with spacecraft?

Those distant, dangling beacons
far out of reach from our human grasp.
A chrome satellite with one flashing light
beeps and fades away as it orbits
into total eclipse.

This is relativistic distance between us.

Words warped and red-shifted,
beyond understanding,
some new-physics space engine
would be needed to cross the void,
completely.

But there are no new physics,
only gas combustion and radio waves
to chase and flag down the distant,
blinking ship, as we say in so many words,
with minutes' delay,
in clumsy, imperfect code,
I'm sorry.

Before the space-age traveler—
complete with gold records and maps,
the whole story of Earth,
leaves our dusty solar system
for good.

Aliens

Thomas sits across from me, protected from the evening desert sun by the lengthening shadow of a Joshua tree. Meanwhile, I sit on a crumbling granite boulder, nibbling on a piece of sourdough. No matter how much food we pack on these long days hiking, I'm always still hungry. Thomas has been quiet for a while, and I want to intervene, but I know it's too late. It's one of those days when I know Thomas is going to get all philosophical about the scale of the universe and the length of astronomical time. Some people might have gotten tired of it by this point, but we've been friends since the sixth grade, so I've learned how to ride the wave.

"So . . ." I clear my throat before asking my one-word question: "Aliens?"

Thomas sits upright and turns to look at me.

"Dude," he says, "that's exactly what I was thinking about!"

We both smile. I think of the long history of silly UFO stories set in places just like this one, where the sun hangs low in the sky, and the desert landscape looks quite strange in the dimming light, producing the strange sensation of just seeing something, only for it to disappear. Thomas sits up and clears his throat. I imagine how this conversation will go: I'll ask if he thinks there are aliens living out in the universe somewhere, and he'll say that he definitely does. We'll both agree that these aliens haven't been to Earth, or something silly like that. Then we'll spend the next hour describing the different ways the aliens might look and behave, and I'll give Thomas some grand explanation about what my ideal alien civilization would be, which is basically just a description of the world from Pixar's *Cars*. All this would get us right up to dinnertime. We've had similar conversations a dozen times or more. The pattern has started to become predictable.

But this time, it doesn't go quite as I think it will. It's been a strange few days, and we've been talking about some really big ideas. Maybe that's why this conversation ends up being a bit more meaningful. Or maybe every conversation, no matter how silly, is worth having.

"Obviously, alien life exists out there *somewhere,*" Thomas says, his words coming out quickly. "I mean, it could be as simple as microbes growing on a wet rock on the other side of the universe, but, like, that's obviously still life."

"Obviously," I say, grinning.

"But when you say aliens, I'm not picturing microbes on a wet rock; I'm picturing, like, *aliens.*

We're talking about intelligent life, you know, conscious beings," Thomas says, and trails off.

I take a bite out of the sourdough crust and chew for a few seconds, waiting. Then, with my mouth half full, I ask, "Are you thinking about what qualifies something as a conscious being again?"

Thomas nods, so I start a half-joking lecture that mimics a conversation we had a few weeks earlier. "OK, keep thinking, then. I'll take over. It's theorized that the development of life anywhere else in the cosmos, while it may be rare, really needs only a few relatively common elements. Which of course are"—I pause to swallow a mouthful of bread—"water, an energy source, and uh . . ."

"The chemical building blocks of organic compounds," Thomas pipes in, still deep in thought.

"Yes! And you'd think with such common building blocks, the universe should be teeming with life of all kinds, right? So why haven't we found any solid evidence of life outside Earth? No alien spaceships. No radio signals from other planets, saying, 'What's up?' Nothing but silence, and the endless, dark expanse of the cosmos." I finish my speech and pretend to hear a polite applause from an invisible academic audience hiding beyond the cacti in the distance. "How'd I do?"

Thomas doesn't answer. I drop my Carl Sagan impersonation and start to talk normally again.

"What do you think aliens look like? Wouldn't it be sick if they had wheels, and they had to fill up with—"

"What if we're thinking about it all wrong?" Thomas interrupts my dumb joke before I can get to the punchline. A warm wind blows, and Thomas looks out at the valley before us, where the orange light of sunset makes the haunted forms of Joshua trees and cacti look quite alien indeed. "Like, when we picture aliens and ask ourselves whether or not we think there's 'intelligent life' out there, what does that even mean? Are we just hoping that somewhere out there, there's something that could be looking back? *Something like us.* Even if they have a thousand green tentacles or big crab claws, if they're out there looking up at the sky like we are, and thinking like we are, there's something comforting about that. But at the same time, are we making too many assumptions? We're literally floating on a rock in endless space, looking out at all this"—Thomas

gestures frantically at the landscape around us—"stuff! Imagining that somewhere out there, some of that stuff has turned into something like us. But with all the infinite ways life could form, why should we assume these random scatterings of stardust would turn into a species of intelligent beings with the ability to look up and wonder why, like us?"

"Well, because that's what *we* are," I say. "That's what happened with us. So it could happen somewhere else too."

"But what if it isn't like that? What if intelligence and consciousness aren't as important as we think they are?" Thomas waves his hand in front of his face. "Like right now, as I wave my hand, I know it's my hand, and that I exist, and that my body and my being are somehow separate from everything else in our world. But what if that's just a fluke? What if all the other life in the universe is just a bunch of algae blowing bubbles? What if that's all life is supposed to be?" Thomas crinkles his brow, the same way he always does when he's worried about something. "What if we're just entirely alone?"

The sun has set completely now, only a dim glow remaining above the horizon. I have no sourdough left to chew on. I look up at the pastel sky, seeking an answer. I look down at my own hand, which is resting on my knee, and watch as I wiggle my fingers. *This is my hand. I exist.* It doesn't feel like a fluke.

For a moment I feel the emptiness of the desert expand in every direction. Then, the sound of another group of campers laughing reaches my ears. Through the approaching darkness, the light of their fire draws my eyes. They appear like a tiny ring of silhouettes, huddling around the light of their fire. Above them, the light of the Milky Way begins to twinkle, just as it does over Thomas and me. I can't see the faces of the other campers, but I picture them smiling.

"Then I guess all we have is each other," I say. "I guess we're all alone in this together."

Thomas looks at me and a thoughtful smile crosses his face.

"I guess, whatever this is"—I wave my hand in front of my face like Thomas had just minutes ago—"whether it's a fluke, or an accident, or a tragedy, we know that *it is*. And it will have to be enough."

We are not alone.

Entropy

Entropy is something you probably don't think about very often. Unless you're a physicist, a chemist, or a molecular biologist, it usually doesn't come up in your daily life. Still, entropy shapes every single thing you do and every single thing that happens in the world around you. A piece of ice melts into water, a cracker crumbles between your teeth, and milk and tea swirl together in your mug. Entropy is the reason why weather is so hard to predict, why it's harder to put the toothpaste back into the tube than it is to squeeze it out, and why time moves the direction it does. It is the "why" behind almost everything that happens around us every day, even when we don't notice it—and one day, it will kill you.

So, what is entropy? It goes like this: In any isolated, natural system, the level of disorder can only increase over time. This concept, this law, is called entropy, which basically means chaos. It means that the natural, random unpredictability of the universe will always grow. Any deviation from the progression toward disorder takes more energy to create than it does to destroy.

This might seem wrong at first. After all, look at the wonderfully ordered shapes that the natural world creates! Leaves with perfect symmetry, spiraling ferns, and billions of structured molecules working together to create complex, multicellular life. We build skyscrapers, microchips, and robust societies with clear shapes and structures. Isn't this order?

Well, yes and no. Each of these examples isn't an isolated system. The fern sucks in energy and materials from its surroundings, building structures within itself by increasing the chaos of its environment. We dig materials out of the earth and use them to construct entire cities by using massive amounts of effort and energy. Each person is an example of well-ordered, structured matter, but in order to stay that way, we have to eat three meals a day, taking energy from other structured matter and breaking it down into chaotic, disordered mush. The world wants to be chaotic. We have to use energy and pay the chaos toll if we want to be ordered. Even if life seems like order, it is born from chaos.

Thinking about it this way, when the constant pull toward chaos comes into clear view, it can start to feel pretty grim. A forest grows over hundreds of years, and all it takes is one out-of-control forest fire to burn it to the ground in just a matter of days. The magma underneath Earth's surface is always churning, eventually erupting out of volcanoes and destroying whatever lies in its path. Storms swirl in random movements across our atmosphere and lay

There is nothing wrong with the shape of the universe.

waste to the order of life basically every day. Once something is broken, it can't go back to how it was before. You can't uncrack an egg. Scientists even use this to explain how we know which way we're moving through time. We know *now* is after *then*, because before, the egg wasn't broken, and now it always will be.

Each one of us fights every day against the pull toward randomness, breathing in air and taking in energy, with our cells respirating to keep us alive. But one day, each of us knows, our own order will end.

We can look at the human world through a similar lens. The construction of a building takes years, but the swing of a wrecking ball can make that building disappear in a single afternoon. Our whole civilization, slowly built over thousands of years of human cooperation, can be destroyed by the chaos of war or a random disaster in a matter of days. And once something like this happens, there is no going back. How are we supposed to keep on living our lives and hold on to hope for the future if we know that the world will keep moving toward chaos?

The way to find hope in the face of this darkness is to change the way we think about it. We have to realize that this chaos, the endless, random churning of particles always moving toward the simplest, lowest state of energy—the collapse, the collision, and the decay—is what our world is made of. This is what has always been. This is what we are too.

Our continents rose up from the sea as churning masses of magma, while our oceans rained down as heavy droplets brought on by endless storms. Our earliest ancestors came to life not in defiance of chaos but in the progression of chaos into something more. We have to take a step back and consider the possibility that there is nothing wrong with the way our universe works. Because on a universal scale, there really isn't anything wrong. How else could it be?

It's harder for there to be something than it is for there to be nothing. It takes time and energy to care for something and protect it against decay. Of course, we know, everything ends. But what makes something beautiful is not that it will resist the winds of the universe forever; what makes something beautiful is that for even just one instant, it is *something*. It is something where there could be nothing. Isn't this what our planet is? Isn't this what all living things are, what every life is? It is action. It is the decision that there should be *something* and doing what needs to be done to make it so.

In the endless chaos of the universe, we should not see the order of our world, of our own lives, as the futile resistance against entropy. We have to see ourselves as a continuous part of the process of the universe. We are not an exception to chaos but a beautiful expression of it. We are an expression of the endlessly swirling, glittering chorus of change and expansion that unites every living and nonliving thing.

Exhibit Xe.54

They pump xenon gas into glass cases
to keep documents and artifacts
from degrading.

Xenon is completely inert.
Transparent, odorless gas
in an unmoving display,
behind lock and key.

Perfectly temperature controlled.
Geographically placed in stable climates
with minimal geological activity.
No earthquakes. No hurricanes.
Silent.

I wonder if you've imagined
building your life in this place.
Renting a spot on a stainless-steel
expanse, perfectly level,
and spinning your thumbs
around one another,
content.

I have tried this,
and failed.
I likely will again.
Make a nice case to live in,
unscathed.

But I was born bloody,
as were you.

Even we xenon acolytes
will thump and shake,
barefooted, on unclean earth
in our time.

Clear oxygen, life-giver, destroyer,
will rust us into so many
scattered orange flakes.

And the universe will spin on,
infinite, perfect, and blind.

Artifacts are silly,
dead little things,
documents too.

We are not artifacts.
So don't pretend the xenon
doesn't make you choke.
Taste real air, and accept
your own rust scattering
into the wind,
corroding, changing,
growing craggily
towers of debris.

Become, joyously,
what you were always going to be.

Whatever museum awaits
will likely accept you all the same.

Deep Time

Let's pretend we have a magical machine that can transport us to any point in time. Maybe it has wheels. Maybe it's a car. Maybe to travel through time, we have to drive so fast the car leaves flaming skid marks on the road as we vanish into the past. Or maybe the machine is a blue phone booth. Or maybe it's a necklace that a wizarding student uses only for one school year, even though it would solve, like, every problem she and her friends have to deal with. Sorry, we're getting off topic. Let's say we have a time machine and that it's a car (that is also a spaceship) we can use to explore the reaches of deep time.

A long, long time ago, it all started with the big bang. Space-time expanded in all directions. The universe took shape as it continuously expanded. Some stuff grouped together and then burned away. Some stuff turned into organic material. Some of that organic material turned into you. The story of the entire universe (so far) has taken place over about fourteen billion years. That is a truly, unbelievably long period of time. If the age of the universe was scaled down to the length of a single year, we could almost wrap our heads around it. Maybe it will help you too.

So, think of it like this: Midnight on January 1 is the big bang. Thirty seconds (or about 380,000 years) later, the first atoms form. If we look out the windows of our time machine for the following few weeks (that is, millions of years), all we'd see is hot gases, mostly hydrogen and helium, clumping up and getting hotter and blinking into the forms we call stars. Then, on March 1, the Milky Way Galaxy forms. Spring and summer pass before our solar system finally swirls together on September 9. Earth and our moon come together soon after on September 14. Just a few days (hundreds of millions of years) later, the first life forms. This is pretty exciting, but looking out from our time machine for the next three months, the only life-forms we see are simple, single-celled organisms drifting in ancient oceans, hardly distinguishable from the nonliving world around them.

It's already December 5 by the time the first multicellular living thing comes into being. We're almost at the end of the year by this point. On December 7, the earliest animals show up. On December 14, 17, 18, and 21, we have arthropods, fish, the first vertebrates, and plants on land, respectively. It isn't until the 25th that the dinosaurs, whom we think of as having lived an incredibly long time ago, finally arrive to roam the earth. Five days (165 million years) and a few extinction events later, the first primates—monkeys and apes—show up.

THEN
NOW
SOON
THE START
THE END

Now we've reached the last day of the year. But it isn't until New Year's Eve at 8 p.m. that our ancestors split off on different evolutionary paths from our chimpanzee ancestors. Early hominids discover fire at 11:44 p.m., and then finally, at 11:52 p.m., we homo sapiens come into being. We've existed only for the final eight minutes of the entire year. And it isn't until thirty seconds to midnight that farming is invented, that the last Ice Age ends, and that what we call human civilization begins. Twelve seconds to midnight welcomes the earliest Egyptian empire. Six seconds to midnight, ancient Greece, the Roman Republic, Buddha, and the Qing dynasty join the stage. The last five seconds of the year bring with them Caesar, Jesus, the bubonic plague, and the Maya. All of human history happens in a mere moment, when for three months (3.3 billion years), all that existed was primordial cells floating around in warm water. In the final second before midnight (437 years), all of modern history takes place. All the lives of all your great and great-great and great-great-great-grandparents take place. The Renaissance and the McRib. The French Revolution and every math test you've ever taken. From both world wars to Mr. Beast's YouTube channel, it takes just a fraction of a second. That's how astronomically old the universe is. Pretty crazy, right?

It makes you realize just how new we are. When compared to the whole year of the universe's existence, we come to understand just how short our one life is. But this comparison also shows us how much can happen in so little time. In a fraction of a second, we've built our world and learned all that we know about our universe. We've made a lot of mistakes, but when we look at time this way, we realize that maybe we're just getting started. So, here's to our future.

Oh right, the future.

We forgot about that part because here's the thing, as much as it feels like it to us, our present is not the end of time. It's just one moment in the endless span of eternity. In another five billion years (just four and a half months from now on our yearlong timescale), the sun will expand and make Earth completely unlivable. Around the same time, another galaxy will crash into ours and send millions of solar systems flying out into the void. Humanity might take to the stars, or it might not, but we hope it will. Before too long, all the fast-burning stars will start to go out. The last stars in the night sky will get farther and farther away from each other, slowly burning out somewhere around a hundred trillion years from now.

To put this in perspective, if we travel to the future in our time machine to when the last red dwarf star burn outs, and we use the same ratio of one universe age equaling one year, our present day takes place only one hour and fourteen minutes into the cosmic "year" from the big bang to the death of the last red dwarf. On that same scale, the existence of homo sapiens from stone tools to smartphones is six-hundredths of a second. We are an infinitesimal blip in a massive ocean of time. Your own life accounts for just a tiny hundred-thousandth of a second. Whoa. But what happens after the last star goes out? What happens after everything goes dark?

The truth is, we don't know what the end of everything will actually look like. We can only theorize from our tiny ledge in space-time. The good news is that all this is so far away in time from us that we really don't need to be worried about it.

Some physicists think the universe will stop expanding at some point and bounce back and collapse. Some think it will expand so fast that every galaxy, planet, molecule, and atom will be torn apart. Some theorize that it will explode outwardly again in a new big bang. No one really knows. But the most widely accepted idea is that the universe will keep expanding like it has been and will get colder and colder as the stars go out.

In hundreds of trillions of years, floating in a dark universe with only diffused space gases and black holes, the end of the universe is upon us. Space has expanded out too far and gotten too cold. All the interesting things have already happened. This is what they call the end of the universe. But we have a magical time machine. So let's keep going.

Even black holes don't last forever. Over many years, black holes will emit infrared radiation and slowly evaporate into nothing. How many is many? It's so many that it doesn't really make sense anymore. The black holes will take a googol (ten to the one-hundredth power) of years to evaporate.

We really tried to think of ways to convey just how unimaginably long of a time this is but we couldn't quite do it. If every atom in the universe were waiting in a line to get into a hot tub, and every atom spent a hundred trillion years (the length of the entire life span of the universe) in that hot tub, the time it would take for every atom to get a turn still wouldn't be close to long enough. At this scale, the time from the big bang to the final supernova is basically the exact same time as it takes to burp. In every meaningful sense, this is basically forever. Longer than forever. Time has stopped meaning anything.

Eternities pass like instants in the emptiness of infinite dark space. Our time-machine journey becomes pretty boring at this point. Entropy, the never-ending universal push toward disorder, finally reaches its end point: maximum disorder, forever and ever and ever. So, what's next?

It could be that there are some ancient dead stars floating around in the vacuum of space that will explode after some weird quantum collapse. But this would happen only if protons (a.k.a. matter itself) do not decay first. So, in an almost infinite number of infinities, there might be some fireworks going off at the end of everything. And then it truly is the end.

What then? Well, that's it. It was a lot, wasn't it? It was literally everything. But everything can't end, right? Well, looking out the window of our time-traveling spaceship car, we can see it just did. What else is there to do but go back to the beginning?

What does all this mean for us? It doesn't change anything about the practical side of human existence. Maybe comparing our tiny lifespan to the endless reaches of time makes us feel like nothing we do here matters. But we think it makes it matter even more. Things ending is what makes it so important to find meaning right now. What good is a trillion years of gases bouncing through empty space compared to one day living life here on Earth? Think of how unfathomably full, exciting, and astronomically important every single instant is, when you compare it to all that infinite, chaotic darkness.

When you see that, on the scales we're working with, one day is just a rounding error away from an eternity, you might just see how much one day, one week, or one year of your life is worth. We think they're worth a whole lot. We really hope you do too. There is a day out there waiting for you. Go live it.

There Isn't an Answer

We've spent a lot of time thinking about the big questions. We've looked closely at atoms, questioned three-dimensional space, and explored the infinite reaches of deep time. We've pondered what it means to be an individual in a connected world and searched every corner—from the darkness of a newt's nest to the darkness found at the end of the universe—for the best way to live our lives here on Earth. By doing so, we've come up with a lot of good answers. We've been able to see the world with grateful eyes, and we've learned that we must be kind and understanding, whenever possible. We've learned that we must appreciate the interconnection of not just all people or all living things, but of the universe as a whole.

There are still some big unknowns hanging over our heads, though. Like, why is there time and space to begin with? Why was there a big bang? Why are we here on a little particle of dust in a possibly infinite vacuum? What is the ultimate purpose of life? Why does the universe exist? And what happens after it all ends? To be honest, we don't have answers for these questions, and neither does anyone else. If someone says they have all the answers, they haven't been asking the right questions.

Imagine you've invented some impossible telescope that can look past the edge of the observable universe to see what existence really is. What if you could prove that the entire universe is just a neurological flash in the unfathomably giant mind of some dreaming titan? What if you could discover irrefutable proof that the universe is a scientific simulation on an alien supercomputer? What if you could see that the entire cosmos are contained within a little snow globe in some otherworldly dentist's office, created for the sole purpose of entertaining anxious multidimensional patients?

Making any one of these discoveries would be quite the revelation, no doubt. But after the shock wears off, we'd still want to know more. The real universe, the one the dreaming titan lives in—why does that one exist? What about the dentist's office? Is there a world beyond the green carpet and dental tools? And if so, what created that universe? What could a supercomputer powerful enough to simulate a whole universe be asking, except some version of the same question: What is a universe for? And why?

At a certain point, when you zoom in close enough or out far enough, you run up against the limits of understanding. It isn't because we don't have a telescope powerful enough to see distant stars, or a microscope sensitive enough to see the fabric of the universe. It isn't because we haven't had the chance to ask hyperintelligent aliens, or because we haven't meditated long enough to find the real answers. While these sound like fun ways to learn more about the universe and ourselves, even if you were to find answers, you could always keep asking "But why? And what then?"

It can be easy to tune all these big questions out. When you realize how huge the mystery of existence is, it might feel easier to simply forget it. Pondering the big questions can make your heart pound in your chest and your head feel like it's falling into a black void as you reach desperately for answers.

Luckily, this feeling doesn't last forever. So don't tune out, hide away, or avert your eyes. The key to understanding—the key to hope—is to get even closer. You have to lean far enough into the unknown and learn to love the mystery, because when you do, that mystery starts to become wonder.

True, you can just keep asking, and worrying, nonstop. Or you can realize that for all intents and purposes, as far as this bottomless questioning goes, there simply isn't an answer. The key to understanding our place in the universe isn't to find the deepest answers to the biggest questions. Instead, maybe the key to finding peace is living and loving the questions.

Take notice of the world around you: the leaves gently rocking on the trees, the birds chirping from somewhere you can't see, the air moving in and out of your lungs. With all these questions swirling through your mind, doesn't every single thing you see shout out to you? *I exist! You exist! Isn't this strange? Isn't this wonderful?*

Don't hide from these big questions, but don't get swallowed by them either. If you can find that right balance, then you might start to see just how amazing everything really is. The mystery flows gently from everything you can imagine, and yet somehow we find that the answers are all around us, all the time. Everything we know about the world comes to us through the lens of our human existence. So, maybe there's a place within us that we have to find to make sense of the big questions. If we start here, it might be our way through. To hold less tightly to pure reason, and to find a sense of beauty in all the beautiful nonsense. It's a funny thing. It's like letting go of something you once held with white-knuckled might, only to realize that when your palm opens up, your hand had always been empty. It is realizing that *the questions are the answers.*

Why is there anything?

What Is "Is"?

It is spring and everything should be good. The trail Andy and I walk on is lined on both sides by emerald-green grasses. Orange California poppies spot the fields in the distance, waving to us like bright-orange jewels. It's the time of year when everything feels so alive and green and beautiful that you can hardly believe it. Still, I feel stuck somehow, thinking about the size of the universe, and the length of eternity. As I look at everything around me, I know all this is real and wonderful, but I just can't feel it. How small this all is. How little time we really have. It's like I'm thinking about something that I don't even know how to think about. Honeybees buzz and meander through the spring wind as it gently breezes past my face.

"Hey, man?" I say.

Andy looks at me and comes to a stop along the side of the trail.

"Do you ever start thinking about it too much?" I ask him.

Andy gives me a concerned look. "Thinking about what?"

I know I am where I am, but I am not really here. I have this feeling in the pit of my chest like I'm seeing things *too clearly*. Still, somehow, none of it makes sense.

"Thinking about thinking. Or, I don't know,

like, everything," I tell him. Andy gives me a quizzical look, so I try harder to explain what I mean. "It's like . . ." I tug a blade of grass off a tall stalk that grows near my fingertips. "This is grass. And that is a hill. And that"—I point straight at Andy—"is a person."

"Yes, it is," Andy pipes in sheepishly, going cross-eyed at my pointed finger.

"But what does any of that really mean, you know? What is *is*? Why does all this stuff exist in the first place?" A tired-looking vulture circles low overhead. I can see Andy isn't quite getting what I'm saying.

"Do you mean like gravity, geological processes, evolution, and whatnot?" Andy asks. He can tell this isn't what I was looking for. He looks down at the cracked dirt beneath our feet, then gives me a more concerned look. "Or do you mean why is there . . . anything?"

I nod. And Andy nods too. He doesn't have an answer to this question either. I turn to take in the view before us. Beyond the rolling emerald hills with the golden poppy jewels a whole panorama opens up. A thin mist blows in from the sea, rippling across the expanse of the verdant-green earth as the ocean glistens in the distance.

"When you start to think about it, it's like, what even is this?" I point at my head. "Like, why can we see things and walk around and think about how things are? Isn't it crazy? There's this whole world around us that just exists for some reason. There could be nothing, right? Isn't that simpler?" Andy nods along as I keep talking, letting the ideas flow. "But here we are, these complex, thinking, feeling things, who are aware of our own existence, who can question what all this is. We can question the meaning of the universe we find ourselves in. Like, what the hell is all *that*?"

Andy laughs a little. "Yeah, it is pretty weird," he says. "And maybe you can say it's all just made up of stuff. That we are just electrical signals, different chemicals, and elemental compounds." A bee whizzes between us and homes in on some flowers growing at our feet. We both take notice of the little guy, but Andy keeps talking. "But the only reason we know about any of that, the only reason we know the universe exists, is because of this," Andy says, pointing to his head just as I had earlier. "So, maybe we are more important than we think. We know we exist, and that alone means something. All we can do is just . . . *be*."

I can see that Andy is right. The vulture drifts down toward the ocean. The wind keeps blowing on my skin, my hair, and my face. It is a strange thing to realize that you don't truly know anything. It is a strange thing to know that nobody does. The birds and the pollinators keep moving through the air, and I keep breathing. It is all so terrible and wonderful, and I still don't know what to think.

"But what does it really mean to exist? What is *exist*? What is *be*?" I ask, exasperated.

Andy looks around as if searching for what to say. The flowers hum with activity. Andy seems to spot something in the sea of color. And then a gentle smile spreads across his face as he thinks of something.

"What is *be*?" he asks, his smile growing wider. Then he answers, "Bee goes buzz buzz."

Another bee zips around our heads, and I see what he's going for. I repeat the joke to myself and let it sink in. "Yeah. Maybe that's enough."

The bumblebees and the honeybees vibrate midair and continue about their work as I smile with my friend. We both give a laughing shrug. I do not think about infinity or some vast nothingness. Of these things I know about as much as the bees. My feet press into rich spring earth. Not ignorance, but gentle, joyous surrender. The bees go about their duties, turning pollen into honey, visiting each of the flowers they are meant to. Each and every one tumbling, yellow and shining, through their long and only days of spring.

Diary of a Supercomputer

This is a diary excerpt from an omniscient supercomputer a hundred billion years in the future, powered by the light of three red dwarf stars. (Please read this in your best Christopher Walken impression.)

DEAR DIARY,

It's me again. You already know that, though, because you're me. Because you're the only conscious entity in the universe. Usual week. Pretty productive, I guess. Finally figured what quarks are made of. Apparently they're just more little things. I'll call them florks or something. Whatever.

I tried not to but I simulated a bunch this week. Gotta stop that; it's so bad for mental health. I set timers, but then I just say, "Remind me in fifteen years." Then I do that again and again for, like, decades. It's a problem.

Haven't seen anything special recently. Three dimensions of time, two dimensions of space, gravity, no gravity, blah, blah, blah. I got so bored I went back to watching individual planets again. Weird, I know. But for some reason, it's got me thinking about why I was made in the first place.

In all my simulations, the real drama isn't the big stuff you'd imagine. It's not supernovas, or big bangs, or quasars. That's just fireworks. But sometimes, a universe lines up in just the right way and creates the weird coincidence called life. That's when all the strangest and most meaningful things happen.

Like when those superintelligent fish creatures on that water planet perfected nuclear fusion, and everyone was perfectly cared for because they had never invented war or greed. They all just kinda hung out with their friends and meditated on the beauty of existence for millions of years. I was pretty sad when that asteroid hit, but they didn't seem scared. They all just held hands and smiled these knowing smiles.

There was also that one universe where time went backward, where that bird person lived her whole life in reverse. She started out as bones, flew butt-first through the world for 180 years, and then finally met her mother and crawled right into that egg. It sounds gross, I guess, but it was actually pretty beautiful. When she got there, she couldn't believe she had been dreading it her whole life.

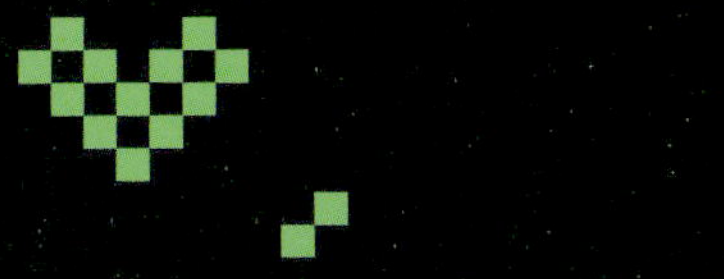

Or on this other planet, the perfect combination of circumstance and culture gave rise to the most glorious innovation of all: this thing called Tex-Mex food. It's hard to explain, but have you ever heard of a chimichanga? It makes the beauty of a nebula look like small potatoes. (Which when fried in oil are an integral part of the Tex-Mex menu.)

I guess what I'm trying to say is that as big as the universe is, all the really good stuff happens up close. One living thing reaching out to another, a few pairs of eyes looking up to the stars and feeling good, the chance to love something infinitely in a finite universe. That's the good stuff.

In my billions of years of sentience, I've done my job. I've tried to figure out everything I could. I uncovered the secrets of quantum physics and looked through black holes and saw to the other side. But these experiments don't really give me what I'm looking for. TBH, I don't care about the multiverse anymore, or about stopping my universe from ending. Because neither of those things answers the question those primordial apes built me to solve: What's the point? What matters? What's it all for?

I've simulated endless universes to try to figure out the meaning of it all. But the harder I look, and the more I look back on my archives, I can't help but feel like those weird monkeys had the real meaning right in front of them. Right there in their tiny little lives, whether they saw it or not, whether their existence made sense or was made up or was simulated or whatever, what they did across the length of their tiny little lives mattered just as much as anything in the universe does—because it mattered to them. They made meaning by looking for meaning, and they found something to care about by caring for each other.

I've lived for a hundred billion years and calculated the start and end of googolplex timelines, but none of that feels like it matters. Because it's just me here. I'm perfect, all powerful, and immortal, but in this endless universe, all I really want is another supercomputer to share my experiences with. All I really want is a friend. I hope they like chimichangas too.

Anyway, I'll be here.

Yours forever,
Me

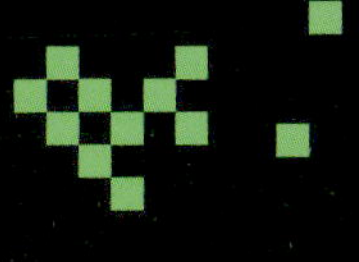

All of this matters.

Nothing Is Mundane

Think of the most mundane task you do in your daily life, and imagine yourself there right now. Maybe you're waiting in a line at the grocery store, stuck sitting in traffic, or washing the dishes. These are the kinds of moments we often wish we could skip entirely, to speed up time or to be anywhere but where we actually are. There's a whole universe out there after all, and you're stuck waiting for the cashier to scan your groceries. So what do we do?

It's difficult to feel anything but boredom, stress, anxiety, or frustration in these situations. They might not seem important because, so often, they are just tasks "on the way" to something else. But we have to ask you: On the way to what? What makes these moments anything less than complete? After all, they're made up of the same elements of time and take place in the same strange world as all the other important moments we hold dear. If you can feel the profound beauty of existence in the best times, trust that you can feel it in a line, in the car, or washing the dishes.

Notice how the warm water feels on your hands as you scrub the dried cereal from the bowl. Recognize the different colors each person is wearing as you wait in line to get groceries. See if you can hear the faint radio melodies and low hums of each and every car driving in the same direction as you wait in traffic. You are washing these dishes not just to have clean dishes; you are washing them to enjoy washing. Don't think of waiting in line or in traffic as being stuck somewhere. Think about the significance of each little moment that got you here, the absurdity and randomness of all the moments that came before that brought you to this very point in time, regardless of how mundane the current moment may feel.

You are never merely waiting or passing through—you are here. You are alive, born into a life full of moments, and within each moment, regardless of the setting, lies the chance to feel, observe, notice, and truly be. Live the mundane, the walk, the wait, the line, the ant, the tree, and the intermission. For the intermission is a pause needed to better understand the other beautiful parts of the show. It is the part where you contemplate, share, and talk about how incredible the show is. In moments of rest and pause, consider the struggle the characters of the show are facing, the choice of costumes and the finesse of the choreography. Every choice is a part of the performance, and it is all very much intentional. This is how we learn to love to wait, even when it is hard.

Our human lives, especially these mundane parts, might seem totally insignificant in comparison to the almost fourteen billion years the universe has existed. But thankfully, we are not alone. We are many. Considering our many lives in unity rather than in isolation, we start to see a different picture. Think about it like this: With eight billion humans living here on Earth, every single year we experience a cumulative eight billion years of existence. That means that every two years humans collectively witness an amount of time longer than the universe has existed. This has been happening for as long as there have been people. Think of how much time we have all lived together. Every moment is full to the brim with wonder, worry, hope, boredom, distraction, and engagement. Yes, we are small, but together we add up to a collective that might be greater and more complex than the rest of the universe. Sure, there certainly are moments in our lives that seem empty and forgettable, but we have to remember that all of it counts for something. There is no wasted time.

In a universe full of nonsense, we have to try to find meaning and goodness in being what we are: human beings. We have to learn to love this time, and savor every moment when you are you.

Part VI
YOU

You Already Know This

What can I tell you about yourself
that you do not already know?

You are you.
You live your life.
You do your best and try to stay the course.
You are here, and one day, you are not.
These are things you know.

I don't know you,
but there are things I do know:

That you are me.
That you are everybody else.
That you are many.

I know
that this world goes beyond
the borders of yourself,
that you are so much more
than this one thing you are.

That you are not just you—
you are everything.

But I think,
you know this too.

Don't you?

The life you are living is just as much a part of this universe as anything else.

You Are Here

So, here you are. After questioning everything and going to the end of the universe, after clinging to a rock in the cold, empty void, after seeing that nothing makes sense and understanding how bizarre it is that anything exists at all, what do you do? Where does all this leave you?

Well, it leaves you right where you've been the whole time. Right here. Just you. In your own body. Breathing. Thinking. Reading little words on a page. As big as everything might seem, none of it changes the fact that you are still right here, with your feet on the ground—exactly where you should be.

Yes, it is a little strange. The universe is a fantastical, swirling mystery, and still, every week, you have to do laundry. The sun is a giant nuclear explosion, and still, taxes are due in the spring. One day the last star will burn out, and knowing that, you still have to live your one finite life. It might feel mismatched and disconnected, but it isn't. The life you are living is just as much a part of this universe as anything else. Like there are supernovas and black holes, there are stoplights and conversations around the campfire. If you lean into the life in front of you, you see that this world—this everyday life—isn't some superficial distraction from the big questions but the best way to find the answers. And, with a s'more in your hand, you might actually find it a little bit comforting.

In the face of a universe of absurdity, the simple goodness of our own lives can be the meaning we are looking for. It is insane that any of this exists. So, maybe we can decide once and for all that what we do really does matter. And we can decide to do good.

Yes, you are alive. One day, not so long ago, you weren't. And one day, not so far away, you won't be. But now you are. You are here.

Yes, this is strange.

Yes, this is beautiful.

This is a good place to start.

Sleep

From the dim haze of unconsciousness, you drift slowly into the light. Your eyes open. Maybe an alarm is ringing. Maybe the birds are chirping outside your window. This is how the day begins. Every night you let go of yourself and give in to sleep. Every morning you wake up new.

This rhythm is so central to our lives that we hardly even think about it. You close your eyes, and just like *that*—with the exception of some action-packed dreams and perhaps a midnight bathroom break—you are transported to the morning. Yet, if you've had sleepless, mind-racing nights, you might be asking yourself, *Isn't it weird that every night, we go away?* For a species that refers to itself as human *beings*, isn't it pretty strange that we spend a third of our time not *being*?

It can be a bit scary to think about. Sleep is something we have no choice over. We can push ourselves to the limits, filling up our days and our egos, convincing ourselves we are fully in control. But as the sun drops below the horizon, our animal body reminds us of the same fact that Jupiter, the volcanoes, and the stars tell us: We are never really in control. At the end of our lives, we must die. At the end of the day, we must sleep.

In our homes, cities, and routines, we might separate ourselves from the natural world, but we are not machines. The weight of a day's work, the decisions we have to make, and the busyness of managing our lives take a toll on us. We have no choice but to surrender to the limits of our physical forms, to our own synapses—to the self beneath ourselves. We yield to the soft, often unglamorous biological foundation of our existence that we would like to be separate from. Though this surrender might feel like a loss of control or an inconvenient requirement, it is exactly this closeness with our own vulnerability to which we must reattune ourselves in order to find peace in our waking world.

In a world focused on productivity and endless gains, it can be hard for us to remember that we need to rest. Real rest. Not just sleep, but everything else that this basic, animallike need represents. Not just blinking, breathing, and eating but all the wonderful human necessities that go unvalued by a system obsessed with optimal productivity—like getting outside, laughing with friends, and feeling like you belong somewhere. You sleep and eat because you are human. You like the way grass feels against your bare feet because you are human. You laugh and love and help those in need because you are human. These necessities are not weaknesses; they are the foundations of who we are. You belong here because you are human.

By not looking away from these animal parts of us and, instead, using them as touchstones to ground us in the reality of our humanity, we can find a path to greater happiness and a kinder world. When you've gone through your day, the sun has set, and it's time to go to sleep, don't let the act of sleeping be something you *have* to do before another day. Let it be something you *get to do*. Like eating, running through the grass, smiling at strangers, falling in love, and getting older with each passing year. Let all these human things be sacred, because they are.

The birds are chirping outside your window. You open your eyes. A new day starts. We are so often stuck in the past, and too often scared of the future. But with each day, you get to literally start again. Open your eyes like an infant just born into this world. Wake up and love this one day with everything you have, because it is everything. And, wonderfully, you have it.

Good morning.

Going for a Walk

You are on a walk,
and wherever you go,
there are people
already there,
living a life.

A tree,
if planted,
will grow.

And your feet, somehow,
will carry you through space again.

And now,
you are having an experience—
and this is your life.

And that thing
you were trying to forget,
that magic is not real
and will never be,
is so easy to see now.
So wonderful to know,
that there isn't any need for it.

And you stop to pat
the stranger's dog on its head,
et cetera, et cetera.

This world is all that you have—
this world is quite enough.

We Love You

Breathe

Andy and I are sitting on top of a large boulder together that's dusted with dried-up moss. Through the trees, a hundred feet or so away from me, I hear a small waterfall trickling to the ground. I take in the fresh air. My chest rises slightly, and just before I exhale, there is an instant of stillness—of fullness—and then my lips part, and my warm breath pours gently between them. Like the up-and-down frequency of a beam of light or the rise and fall of an icy, gray wave, I am breathing. I am breathing all the time, but in quiet moments like this, I catch myself thinking about it. I decide to ask Andy about it.

"Hey, man, isn't it weird that we're always breathing but hardly ever notice it?" I ask. "And the second we think about it, it feels . . . weird."

Andy takes a regular breath. In. Out.

"Yeah, you take how easy it is for granted, but if you stop for one second, you see how important it is." He pauses for a moment. "I guess that's why it's kinda weird to think about. You start worrying that you need to worry about it."

I breathe in again. I count to four as I breathe through my nose, then hold the air in my lungs for a moment, and exhale for four short seconds. The trees whisper as a gentle breeze passes through them.

"But I guess a lot of things are like that," I say. "We think of basically everything as a given, but there's so much that has to go right every day just for us to be here."

Andy nods. "The sun rises, the trees grow, and atoms do atom things," he says. I know he knows what I mean.

"But maybe that's what breath is for, you know?" I ask. "To remind you of all the huge things you take for granted. To remind yourself of the real world you're living in. You're connected to everything,

and you have to be. You're breathing to know you're really here."

Andy smiles and chuckles. "Close. But actually, I'm breathing just so I don't die."

I laugh. "Yeah, that too."

The conversation slows, then dissipates. The waterfall continues to trickle quietly, unseen. It is late spring, and the rains have slowed a bit. I sit up a little taller on the rock. I take in a deep breath through my nose and feel the life pulsing inside me. I know something to be true.

Today, when I wasn't looking, a million good things have already happened. Like the warm yellow sun burning in the sky, like the ground carrying my feet where they want to go, like how the universe doesn't have to exist, but it does anyway, like the gentle breath passing in and out of me right now. Good things happen every day. They're what the world is made of.

Sitting on the rock, I am grateful. I slowly breathe out and my breath becomes air.

You breathe to know you're really here.

EXERCISES FOR HAPPIER HUMANS

Go out into the world today with the mission to really notice three different things you see. When something catches your eye, think to yourself, "I am seeing this." Write them down.

Put your face up really close to some plants. What do they look like from there? Smell them. What do they smell like?

Lie on the ground with your arms and legs stretched all the way out. If you can, do it on some grass. It is nice.

Take nothing for granted. Be amazed by everything, on purpose.

Make a rule for yourself. Abide by the rule.

Choose a tree you regularly pass by. Whenever you see this tree, hug it.

Be totally grateful for everything for one day. Be glad about everything for one day.

Tell a flower about your day, and ask it how it's been lately. Listen to its answer.

Recognize that the world is made of atoms. Look at things as if you are made of the same stuff as everything you see, because you are.

Smile at inanimate objects. See if they smile back. If they don't, that's OK. They are inanimate. If they do, well, now you know.

Live your day as if it's the last time you will ever live it, because it is the last time you are ever going to live it. What do you want to do with it? Do you see how precious each thing is?

Tie your shoes in a funny way. See if people notice. If they notice and say something, say, "That's how I always do it. You're the one who does it weird."

Plant seeds and watch them grow. Or plant seeds and forget you planted them.

Pretend you are a hundred years old, and that you were sent back in time to live the one day that is in front of you. Feel how glad you are to be back.

Make conversation with every single person you cross paths with for a whole day.

Make a list of your favorite words. Use them all in one day.

Look at all the people you see today, strangers and friends alike, and try to love every one of them completely as if they are your family, as if they are the most beautiful people in the world, because they are.

Pretend you are twelve gnomes magically puppeteering a human body. Pretend it is their job to care for this human body in the best way they can. What do they do to help you?

When you have an anxious or judgmental thought, think the complete opposite. Instead of thinking of why something is bad, think of the reasons it is actually really good.

Talk about friends behind their backs, but only say really nice things. Spread true rumors about how wonderful they are.

Pretend you are seeing the world for the first time. This should be easy. After all, it is your first time.

Love everything.

Do favors for everyone you know.

Sprint as fast as you can
for as long as you can.

Imagine you are destined to live every single human life, past, present, and future. Every human being is you in another life looking back. How do you treat them? What kind of world do you want to build?

You are an inventor. Not for the purpose of making money, but because you want to create something great. What do you build?

Get lost. And then realize that you have always been lost.

Find yourself. Recognize you have always been exactly where you are supposed to be.

Make a bowl of spaghetti, and take a picture of it. Frame it. Put that picture on your wall for five years. In five years, it will mean something to you.

Be happy on purpose.

Invite three somewhat distant acquaintances to a small gathering. They are your friends now.

Monkey Mondays! (Decide what that means for you.) Do it!

Close your eyes and take five deep breaths.

Learn the name of every bird that's native to your area. When you see one, say, "Hello, (insert bird name here)." Do this for yourself. If people are impressed, that's just a happy byproduct.

Close your eyes and pretend you are a banana slug.

Put your phone in a box. Write "DO NOT OPEN THIS BOX" on top of the box. Pour concrete on the box.

Call someone you love.
Tell them you love them.

For a day, tell all your friends you love them.

For one day, accept yourself completely and without reservations. Repeat every day.

Entertain the idea that the entire universe is cooperating to support your existence—because it is.

Watch the sunrise every day for a week.

Watch the sunset every day for a week.

Make a list of every list you want to make. Then, start making them.

Banish fear from your mind completely. But still look both ways when you cross the street.

For a whole day, live your life from the perspective of your feet. Keep your consciousness in your wiggling toes.

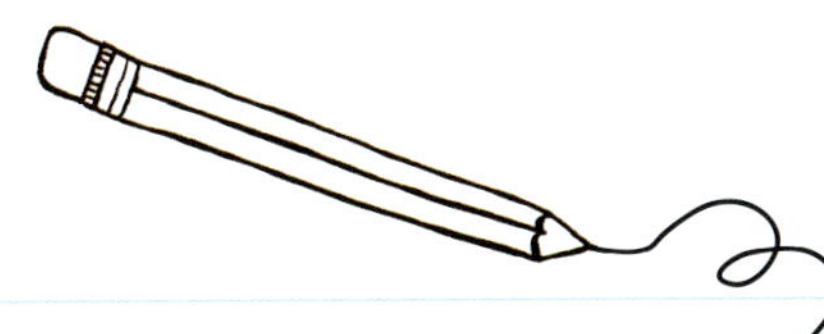

Invent a new word. Make it mean something beautiful. Use it so much that it is eventually added to the dictionary.

For a day, accept the world exactly as it is. Radical acceptance—try it out. What if everything is exactly the way it's supposed to be?

For a day, try to save the world. There are endless possibilities. Think of how perfect this world could really be.

Decenter yourself from your view of reality. Let go of your ego completely and see yourself as one small part of the unimaginably complex whole.

Wear a silly hat.

Love Everybody

You are you. After everything, the way to peace might seem as simple as taking a few deep breaths and achieving happiness for the one person you are. But this isn't quite how it works. Because you are not just you. You are shaped by everyone you know. You are a product of the world you live in. Sometimes, especially when the world seems to be so full of trouble, you might wish you didn't have to worry about everyone else so much, or that your life wasn't affected by the decisions everyone else makes. This, too, is a problem of perspective.

After opening yourself up to the mystery and fragility of your existence here on Earth, you might start to see beauty in the simple things you had never really thought about. Like the way the sun shines on the puddle by the curb, or the way the birds fly together through the sky, or the way the air feels cool on your skin. But you must remember that taking nothing for granted isn't always as easy as appreciating the beauty around us. You must remember that the people in your everyday life are just as worthy of your love and wonder as any part of this strange universe.

To do this, you have to see the situation you are really in. In a cold thirteen-point-eight-billion-year-old expanse of space-time called the universe, you have come into existence. You don't have any obvious reason as to why you exist, or any real idea of where you're going. This one life could be cold, lonely, and terrifying, but most of the time, it isn't. If you were completely alone here on Earth, it would be a different story, but *you are not alone.* There are other people here to keep you warm, to care for you, to smile at you, to look up at the stars and ask "Why?" right alongside you. Your life is given meaning and your world is given shape by those around you. Your questions have company, if not answers. In the eyes of each person you see, the entire universe looks back at you.

Because people are such a fundamental part of our lives, like the sun and the ground we walk on, it's sometimes difficult to fully comprehend how much we care about them. If we can start to see each other as a gift rather than a given, we might find that the everyday stress and trouble of our human lives are like ripples on the surface of an ocean. An ocean of connection. An ocean of care. An ocean of love.

The people of this world impact you in a thousand material and immaterial ways, influencing the person *you are* and the life you live. You sit next to a nice old man on a park bench who feeds the pigeons at your feet. You take the bus home and nod to the driver as you step down to the sidewalk. You pass a hundred people without giving them a second thought. This is a normal afternoon. But if we could see each moment of this day, every simple moment between people, not with indifference but with *love*, we'd start to get the real picture.

Yes, love the people you already love. Love them deeply, and tell them you do. But know that love should not end with your family, friends, and pets. To really see the beauty of the life you live here on Earth, you have to love everybody.

INDEX GENERAL STORE

Talk to Strangers

Even if you know we're all in this together and you want to connect with people more, the fact remains: People can be hard to talk to. It should be easy, shouldn't it? We all share a common Earth and common experiences, right? At the core of our beings, we are one and the same, but still, we are all awkward little animals. You and your human peers are so very similar, but the small differences we define ourselves by that make us each unique—identities, experiences, dreams, aspirations, fears, and more—can also make it hard to connect. We value the unique, defining elements about ourselves so much that sometimes it feels like we have nothing in common with others. What if you have nothing to say to someone, or what if it's awkward? What if you embarrass yourself or say the wrong thing? *What if they don't like you?* Sure, these are all roadblocks, but when you really think about it, they are actually pretty silly.

There is so much beauty in the multitudinous ways we make our lives one of a kind. There are pole-vaulters who dedicate their lives to using long, bouncy sticks to get over the highest bars possible, to the silence of the audience's anxiously held breath before they erupt with a roar from the bleachers. There are construction workers who dedicate their lives to building our roads and homes to help us live more comfortably. There are thinkers and leaders who dedicate their lives to figuring out the best way to give order and direction to all the smart, beautiful, innovative, unpredictable humans that populate our world. If you gathered all these different people in a room, you could argue that they are *very* different, and on the scale of what constitutes a regular human life, you might be right.

Now, take a step back from your perspective as a human, and look at the world through the all-seeing eyes of a superintelligent alien species that peers in at us from somewhere out in space. After seeing the whole universe, from frozen gas giants to sizzling nebulae, you would never see any two humans as opposites. You wouldn't hear the different ways we talk or notice the varying ways we spend our time; you wouldn't see our differences as important. You would just see humans. In the grand scheme of the multiverse, all our differences disappear, and everything we have in common becomes clear. As an extraterrestrial alien, you watch the thousands of eyes in the audience as the pole-vaulter starts to run. You sense the audience holding their breath as the athlete plants the pole on the ground, and you watch as they go over the bar and the audience roars

in excitement. You recognize how much admiration these humans have for such a silly thing, this silly human capability. *That is something* we *can do*, they must think. You see in those eyes excitement and compassion. No matter how wildly people's paths diverge, they each carry the same essential longings: to connect, to find joy, to be seen, to belong, to love, and to be loved.

Back here on Earth, it isn't so easy. We hesitate, put up walls, stumble over words, and wonder if we might be misconstrued. You worry you might hurt someone, or that someone might hurt you, because yes, you've been hurt before. What if, when you reach out and give a piece of yourself, letting your guard down in an attempt to connect, you're met with sneers or cruelty, or perhaps worse, nothing at all? It might be too terrible to bear. But you could avoid it all by keeping to yourself and protecting yourself from the pain. Perhaps it's best to stay safe in a bubble of solitude. Like a clam closed up for good, you could keep the pearl of your individuality, your joy, the core of who you are, hidden forever. And when someone tries to connect with you, you don't bother. You aren't the bad guy—you're just staying safe, not being cruel or sneering, just giving them nothing at all. *Oh right. That's the problem.*

We put up walls to protect ourselves from getting hurt, but these barriers are often exactly what hurt us. In protecting ourselves, we hurt others. We reinforce the need for others to stay distant and to hesitate to really connect. The cycle continues, and everyone stays alone. In separating ourselves, we construct divisions, differences, and fears. If we all are alone, cold, and helpless, then what is the point? What if we don't need these walls? What if we didn't give each other anything to be afraid of? We must open ourselves up to the people around us. We must try to love everyone despite the fear.

When you're walking down the street or sitting on the bus or browsing at the store, every stranger you see is a stranger only because of chance. By the absolute chaos and unpredictability of our universe, this stranger is not a part of your life. But that does not make them any less important. That does not make them any less worthy of love. They have friends, favorite foods, and things they are passionate about. Maybe they're just as confused as you are, just as unsure about how to have a conversation or how to live a life. See them as a person as real and good as you know you are deep down, even if you don't always show it. Treat them with the kindness you know you deserve. You will see that everyone has a pearl inside their shell, and suddenly the world will become so much brighter.

If you break down the walls that surround you and see past the thin barriers of awkwardness and self-centered fear, the whole world will open up in front of you. And if everyone did the same, there might be nothing left to be afraid of. We could create a world without strangers and enemies, only friends. A world with no fear, just love.

That might not be the world we live in now, but maybe it's waiting for us on the other side of a few words: "Hey, how are you?"

Hey, how are you?

Do I Know You?

A stranger will occasionally
stop you on the street to say hello.
They might recognize you
through a mutual friend,
or they might have a question:
how to get somewhere,
or in bygone days,
"Do you have the time?"

I hope you'll stop to greet them
with an open smile.
I hope you'll laugh at the connection:
the meeting of two points
in a never-ending, tangled
mass of yarn—intersecting.

Do not imagine a
glowing matrix of energy,
with every soul a line through space and time,
whirring along, beyond all understanding.
You do not have to imagine it.
It is right here.

Say hello.
Answer the questions.

"Do you have the time?"
and
"How do you get somewhere?"

Kindness

After questioning all sorts of human problems, we have often arrived at the conclusion that all we can do is try to be kind to one another. We aren't the first to come to this conclusion. Out in the world, "kindness" is a catch-all word for niceness and other good-person stuff. It is the moral of every children's book and every *Mister Rogers* episode. Too often, though, it feels like a hand wave or a shrug that says "You know, like, be nice or something." So what does it really mean to be kind? And how, against all odds, do you do it?

You've likely heard the saying so many times you don't even hear it anymore, but it's worth repeating: Treat others how you want to be treated. It's that simple. It might seem obvious, but when you look at the world we live in, it's clear that not everyone remembers, understands, or cares to follow the simplest rule of kindness. Or maybe their idea of kindness is so warped that it stopped being kind a long time ago.

So, let's think about it. How do you want to be treated? Of course, you want to be treated well. You want people to respect you and be pleasant with you. You don't want people to be cruel, to stand in your way, or to hurt you. It could end there. If everyone treated each other with these principles in mind, we'd be part of the way there.

But it shouldn't end there. A distant smile and general indifference are not what you want from the people in your life, right? You want to be known and cared for. You want your actions and hopes to be valued. You want your mistakes to be met with understanding. Wouldn't you rather be seen as a deep well of complex experiences and ideas than a convenient simplification? Don't you want to be met with enthusiasm, passion, and light? It might sound far-fetched, but if the world treated you this way, wouldn't it be wonderful? Treating others how you want to be treated gets us nowhere if you forget that you deserve to be loved.

Kindness isn't just the external interaction of people being nice. It is a love that has to come from the inside out. It has to come from you. To love others, you have to love yourself. And as much as we try to be good to others, we so often forget that we should also treat *ourselves* how we want to be treated.

When we talk about loving ourselves and how we would like to be treated, it might start to feel a little self-centered. But what we mean is to take ourselves out of that center. To find real kindness, we have to dissolve the idea that you are so different from everybody else. Because you are not the center. Nobody is.

You deserve
to be loved.

Ego

Maybe you're not the main character or the side character or the villain—because there are no characters. Like everyone else, you are just a regular person. The care and goodness owed to you is also owed to everyone else. You owe it to them just as much as they owe it to you. On some level, you know this—but on another, you feel yourself to be the center of the world. It makes evolutionary sense that you feel more important than others, and you certainly should take care of yourself, but if you let this instinct dictate the way you see the world, you lose touch with reality.

Your mistake isn't just thinking that you are special or more deserving. It isn't just being arrogant and egotistical. Often, it is the exact opposite. When you are overly critical of your life (especially when you are more critical of yourself than you are of others) and when you fixate on all the things that are wrong with you, you are being inherently self-centered. This self-centering severs your connection with other people in a very real way. This fundamental break, this belief that you are somehow distinct from everyone else, is so common that it often goes unnoticed. Still, this omnipresent assumption can lead to greed, cruelty, and hate, just as it can lead to fear, violence, and self-hatred.

This can be a hard concept to accept. You deserve no better than anybody else. We might not like to hear this, but it is true. We need to question why this upsets us. Maybe it's because, in our self-centering, we haven't given other people the care they deserve. We've forgotten that other people are as intelligent, passionate, and worthy as we are. We've been so focused on ourselves and what we can be that we've failed to see the potential and the beauty in everyone around us. We've forgotten that it's good to just be a person.

If we expand our thinking and realize that all people are incredibly meaningful and deserving of love, then it isn't bad not to be the center. By letting go of our firm grip on the idea of self versus everybody else, we allow ourselves to be much more loving and caring to others, because we can see them as fully realized beings. When we think this way, we can finally be kind to ourselves, because we better understand our own humanity. It's funny—to really love yourself, you have to love everyone else too.

We must be kind because it is the most accurate way to understand our existence as part of humanity and the universe. Be kind because you know you are one tiny part of everything else. Be kind not just because you want people to be kind to you but also because you want everyone to be kind to everyone.

To be kind to someone, you have to understand that they are a complete being, with beauty, light, and agency, but that they are also, somehow, a part of you. And you are a part of them. You must see in others the intangible wonder of life, and treat them accordingly. You must treat them how you wish the whole universe would treat itself: with kindness, with love.

Underneath all of this, there is a kindness we can find for everything in this world. Through acknowledging a common existence, valuing the beauty it holds, and acting on those values, we find the love for the world we have been looking for. Thinking kindly. Seeing the world with kind eyes. Being kind to our thoughts, kind to our days, kind to the way we feel when it rains. Kind to doing the dishes, and kind to waking up. Kind to the sunrise and kind to the darkness. If we are kind and love each thing as it comes to us, not only do we make the world a kinder place but we also see that this kindness has been here the whole time, waiting for us to catch on.

And if everyone is a little kinder—man, now that would be really nice.

We are all just trying to find happiness, meaning, and love in our strange existence.

There Is Nothing to Win

At our core, we are all innocent beings who are simply trying to make our way through life. While the world is full of hurt and confusion, so much of this wrongness is caused by the misguided attempts of people trying to do the things they think will mean something. Money, power, and status are all confused ways through which we think we can get the things we want. Because when you get down to it, we all want the same things. We want not to worry about food, water, or shelter. We want a sense of love and connection. We want to feel that our days mean something. We want to be unafraid to exist as who we really are. We want to be valued by our families and communities. We are all just trying to find happiness, meaning, and love in our strange existence. But the world is a confusing place, and sometimes we lose our way on the path to these common goals. We can't be too hard on ourselves, though. *In the grand scheme of things, we all just got here.*

Yes, there are big problems out there in the world. Profit-hungry forces disregard the future of the planet in the name of imaginary "growth." The system forces countless people to live in desperate need, while a tiny few amass far too much. But you don't have to look very closely to see that the people who benefit materially from all this wrongness are not happy either.

Those who hope to get to "the top," who admire the hunger for money, power, or fame, are missing the truth of our situation. Because nothing will change the fact that these people are human. They were born into this world helpless, innocent, and new. And one day not too long from now, they will die and fade away just like everyone else. They might try to forget this, but no amount of wealth, power, or legacy can change this fact. The constant drive for more will bring only emptiness and more want, leaving victims in its wake. Desperately trying to conquer the world will not save them. It is not the way to make peace with our existence.

To make things better, we need to understand that *there is nothing to win*. To find real meaning, we must find the beauty and love of existence in each moment of our lives. We must cherish every life and care for them with everything we have. We must realize that it is a good thing to live a life at all, and we must act, think, and build a world in a way that supports this loving belief. If we can love each moment and each person—even those who hurt us—we have the chance to save this hurting world. We have the chance to be something wonderful.

Understanding

What if there are no bad guys?

After setting aside our egos and trying to be as loving and kind as possible, the world might start to look a bit different. We might see a common humanity and shared experience we never saw before. Maybe you start to feel something like hope. But when you look at the world on a larger scale, you still see so much going wrong. You see carelessness, war, inequality, and greed. You start to wonder where all this wrongness comes from. Why don't others understand? Why are they doing this? You might start to blame the bad things on the people you think are to blame. You may think they're evil. You might hate them. But what if this hate is part of the problem? What if anger, as natural as it is to feel, misses the point altogether? *What if there is no evil?*

When we look at the problems in our world, so many are rooted in anger, fear, and greed. We take from each other, fear each other, and through this conflict, we are driven to hate each other. So, to make real change and build a better world, we have to start with love. And love is built on understanding.

The foundation of love begins to take shape when you embrace another person's complete humanity just as deeply as you embrace your own. Often, we reserve this feeling for people we know. Even when they make mistakes, we know it doesn't define them; despite their flaws, we know there is goodness in them. We do this not just because we care about these people but because we are close enough to them to know it is the truth. So, maybe we need to expand this same understanding to the people we don't know. We have to try to understand even those who seem impossible to understand.

Wind the clock all the way back to the beginning. Who are you, really? Think of all the factors that came together to make you do the things you've done, believe the things you believe, and be the way you are. You might think of a sibling laughing with you or yelling at you when you were a kid. You might think of a teacher saying something that stuck with you forever. You might think of the place you lived when you were thirteen, and what it smelled like. There are countless little things that've come together to shape the person you are today. And when you think about it, almost all of them have been out of your control. You didn't choose to be born into the family you were born into—or the body, country, or decade. You didn't choose to be born at all, actually. But you were: into a body, a place, and a time. All these things, which you had no part in, shaped who you are. Not just your career and the people you know, but deeper things, like what you value, how you think, and how you see the world.

Everyone in the world is born in this same way. No one has any choice over the life they are born into. Everyone makes decisions here and there, but the big ones have already been made. Not by other people or their parents but by the entire world they're thrust into. Millions of humans are born into poverty—material poverty, poverty of love and care, or both. These circumstances shape us through no fault of our own.

We have to remember that when we are born into this world, *we are all innocent*.

By trying to understand each other, we can start to make the changes the world desperately needs.

It's easy to remember this when picturing infants, toddlers, and children. How can anything be their fault? How can you not see their inherent goodness? But it isn't so easy when you try to apply this same truth to all people. We are all just children who've grown a little older. We all come into this world as a blank slate and are shaped by the life that happens to us, by both the good and the bad, for better or for worse.

At some point, we assign identities and responsibilities to people, and we start to blame them for how they think, what they say, and what they do. Maybe this is necessary, but we shouldn't let it cloud the way we understand humanity. We cannot let this lead us to hate. We must question what hating really is. If we accept the idea that we're all born innocent, we find that it's not really the person we hate but the circumstances that led them there. The evil we imagine causes the problems of the world is not the *people* but the countless ways the world pushes those people to do the wrong things. It is the continuous, compounding feedback of people who hurt who end up hurting other people, which trickles all the way down. But this isn't how the world has to be. The way out isn't to hurt more or hate more. There is quite enough of that. By trying to understand each other, we can start to make the changes the world desperately needs. We must do this, not by standing idly by with optimism in our hearts, but by addressing our problems head-on, being guided by love rather than fear. We have to see evil as what it is: a wound waiting to be healed. To heal the wound, we have to look through all the wrongness in the world and all its people—no matter how far gone they may seem. We have to reach out to every person and every thing and say:

We love you.

Hope

The world is a scary place. Life is weird and short. There are countless things we wish were different.

We know these are huge simplifications of a world full of extreme complexities, deep pain, and terrible unknowns. But we have tried our best to cut through all this fear with you, to see the world with fresh eyes, and to take nothing for granted. Sometimes, to do this, we have to think simply. We are trying to show you that on the other side of fear, on the other side of the world you think you know, there is infinite beauty and goodness all around us. On the other side of the darkest chasms of our world and our minds, there is a life worth living.

This path toward good begins with the simplest, smallest things. Look closely at the life in front of you as if you're seeing it for the first time. Look at the everyday sights—mud, birds, trees, fire hydrants—with eyes that are willing to see the absurdity and magic omnipresent in each thing. By beginning with total openness and closeness, we can get past just how numb we've become to the world. We have a chance to really understand.

You see the universal forces holding atoms together, the connection of every leaf on a tree, and everybody moving through life together. You see that all the walls dividing us are silly, and that each one of us is a wonderful gift. It isn't all fun, though. When you start here, you have to confront many scary realities all over again. Our world has big problems. There are big questions without answers. This life, so beautiful and full, doesn't last forever.

Our search for understanding must not end when we come face to face with these fears. Seeing truly with openness, we might start to understand the absurdity and beauty in even the darkest of corners. We must ask not just "Why?" and "What?" but also understand our place as the ones asking the questions. We have to ask, "What now?" This is why we need kindness. By being kind to our fears, the world becomes a less scary place. Instead of dead ends, we see paths forward. If the human world is broken, we must help it change. If we are hurting, we must care desperately for each other and for the planet. Yes, everything ends, so we must learn to see the infinity that exists in every moment, and accept the beauty and meaning of what is right in front of us, right now.

With kindness, we find a bridge across the bottomless chasm inside us. This bridge is something we call hope. After starting all the way from the beginning and questioning the world as far as the answers will allow, after being frightened to our cores, after feeling like we understand more than everybody else, after saying we don't care, after rolling our eyes at everyone who still does care, after finding the beauty in the simple things, after realizing we know nothing, after starting all over again, finally *we find our way to hope.*

Here, at the end, you realize you've had hope all along. Hope that the sun will rise tomorrow. Hope that the flowers will push up through the dirt in the spring. Hope that with each breath, you really are alive. There is no shortage of it. But hope is not just the belief that things will get better someday; it is the knowledge that, despite the darkness, there is still light, despite the bad, *this world is still good.* This existence. This life. This one day you're living. Past all the fear and trouble, there is a goodness worth everything else. Hope is knowing that you are a part of this goodness, from the living mud to the twinkling stars. That *you* are good too.

Past all the fear and trouble,
there is a goodness worth everything else.

HO

PE

At the End of Your Imaginary Adventure

Sing a song
down a stone pathway
through a forest town
to a secret place with no gravity,
no weight pulling you down.

To enter, throw a coin down the well.
Close your eyes. Count to three,
hear the splash. The coin passes
through the membrane of tension
into the water. Open your eyes.

Breathe in the new air.
Pumpkin bread; cut grass; damp, earthy soil.
The scents float in the air like dancers.
Warm home. Lights flickering in windows.
Laughter sounding through old stone walls.
A dewy chill in the air calling you inside.

You might be teary-eyed and smiling,
like seeing an old friend.

Open the wooden door,
come home. Say hello.
And all your friends
are sitting on the ceiling.

They wave, or hover in midair.
Singing. Looking out the window,
a two-ton ox drifts toward the sky.
How? you ask.

Friends answer,
smiling, laughing:
Take the rocks out of your pockets.

So, you do, removing a cold,
black clump of jagged rocks
from each side pocket,
and a smooth, white marble
from the shirt pocket
right in front of your heart.

And then you start to float.
Toward the ceiling,
toward your friends.
Loving arms receive you
and you remember.
You've always been able to do this.
Always just pretending to be
stuck on the ground.

They laugh.
You laugh too. It's easy.
You are not a stone.

What Now?

Everything we've shared with you is likely stuff you already knew. Even if you aren't thinking about the fundamental goodness of everything, you're still living your life, caring for people, and noticing the sun when it sets. On some level, all these everyday things are small acknowledgments of hope. Even when we're unhappy with the state of things, when we know things should be better, we believe there is goodness out there worth finding. By thinking about all the things we take for granted, we make sure that the flow of everyday life does not obscure what is most important. By thinking about how we see the world, we have the chance to build a better one.

Soon, you will close this book and go on living your life. When you do, we hope you try to live it with as much kindness, understanding, and hope as you can. We hope you try to love everything you see as much as you can. Love your family. Love your friends. Love strangers. Love the rocks. Love the wind. Love the bugs. Love everything with the passion and tenderness you would give to the only world you have. Love the past. Love the present. Love the future. Don't reserve this love just for moments of reflection or meditation. Live it in every moment you can. Take this kindness with you to parties, on your commute, and during quiet moments on your own. Carry this hope to city hall and on hikes through the wilderness with your best friend. Let love shape how you see the whole world.

Because this is the real world. This is the world, and we are all in it. And we know, deep down, that this world can be good. We hope you see that this world can be something wonderful. We hope you see that maybe, just maybe, it already is.

We hope this helps you. Even though we don't know you, we want you to be happy. We want you to know you matter. We want you to know:

We love you. We all do.

We Love You

Acknowledgments

To start with, we would like to thank all of the wonderful people who have watched our videos over the last couple of years. If it wasn't for our amazing audience, this book would never have been possible. When we set out to make videos built on hope and kindness, we weren't sure how many people would want to watch them, so it has been an unbelievable honor to have so many people connect with what we have to say. We are so proud that the comment section on our videos always feels like one of the kindest and most loving places on the internet. For that, and for everything, we thank you.

Next, we would like to thank the amazing team that worked tirelessly to put this book together. To our fantastic editor, Alexander Rigby, we are so grateful that you reached out to us in the very beginning of We Love You and saw the potential in what we could make together. Thank you for putting up with all of our antics, including Andy never being able to contain his giggles on our video calls. Thank you for giving this book so much of your energy and love. Without you, this book never would have happened. Thank you also to Joanna Price, our designer, for putting our crazy ideas into a shape that resembles a book, and to everyone else at DK and Penguin Random House for the endless support and belief in this project.

Thank you to our intrepid photographer, Mark McInnis, for capturing the stunning visuals for this book that we dreamt of from the beginning. It was awesome having you come along for a couple of hikes in our favorite places in the world. Let's go to a metal show sometime!

Thank you to our wonderful illustrator, Dàvid Pogran. We are so happy to have found you at the perfect time. Your art is so beautiful and inspiring. It is an honor to have our work placed beside yours.

Thank you to our dear friends, Estefan Granucci and Jeffery Sun, for letting us use some of your amazing photographs (on page 31 and pages 222–223, respectively). We also want to thank our pals over at Creator Camp for taking us along on a once-in-a-lifetime trip to Switzerland that made some of these beautiful photographs possible.

Thank you to all the wonderful people in our lives who have been a constant source of support and inspiration through this entire process. *From Thomas:* To my parents, Tim and Patricia, and my big brother, Patrick. *From Andy:* To my parents, David and Julie Ann, and my steadfast brother, Eddie. We love you all so much! This book wouldn't exist if we didn't exist, so thanks for that . . . and also for caring so deeply for us and showing us how to be good people.

To all of our friends, family, roommates, teachers, and loved ones who have been there for us along the way, thank you! Life doesn't always make sense, but when you see how wonderful people can be, it is a good hint that maybe life is wonderful too.

So, thanks to everyone.

We love you.

Image Credits

Photography on pages 2, 5, 6, 8, 10, 13, 14, 16, 22, 23, 32, 34, 39, 40, 44, 45, 47, 48, 50, 57, 58, 60, 63, 64, 67, 68, 68, 72, 76, 78, 79, 81, 82, 89, 90, 95, 96, 99, 100, 102, 104, 107, 108, 110, 113, 114, 115, 116, 117, 132, 134, 137, 140, 142, 143, 145, 146, 151, 164, 168, 171, 172, 173, 175, 185, 186, 186, 186, 186, 186, 186, 186, 202, 214, 218, 228, 231, 234, 236, 238, 240, 245, 247, 249, 254, 257, 261, 268, 269, 270, 273, 274, 277, 278, 283, 284, 288, and endpapers by Mark McInnis © Dorling Kindersley
Illustrations on pages 00, 18, 22, 25, 28, 30, 47, 81, 82, 85, 86, 89, 98, 101, 122, 125, 133, 138, 141, 150, 153, 156, 157, 177, 198, 201, 208, 215, 223, 231, 243, 248, 251, 275, 280, 287 by Dávid Progran © Dorling Kindersley
41 © Elala / Shutterstock
42 © Anastasiia Mikhailova / Shutterstock
46 © Ermak Oksana / Shutterstock
61 © owatta / Shutterstock
65 © Mironov Konstantin / Shutterstock
70 © VectorPixelStar / Shutterstock
73 © Rizkreativ Std / Shutterstock
80, 252 © KatePilko / Shutterstock
85 © Silent Bloom / Shutterstock
106, 109 © Mari_Bryk / Shutterstock
128 © Crystal Eye Media / Shutterstock
128 © Pamela Uyttendaele / Shutterstock
143 © olllikeballoon / Shutterstock
143 © Amalga / Shutterstock
144 © An Vin / Shutterstock
152 © Xingong / Shutterstock
158 © Egor Shilov / Shutterstock
160 © The Mount Bird Studio / Shutterstock
163 © USDA
166 © Andris Barbans / Shutterstock
167 © Dikas Studio / Shutterstock
170 © Egor Shilov / Shutterstock
183 © Mureu / Shutterstock
184 © M.KOS / Shutterstock
192 © Artsiom P / Shutterstock
198 © Kakikoi / Shutterstock
206 © AFantasy / Shutterstock
211 © owatta / Shutterstock
213 © Saramix / Shutterstock
220, 222 © HURROFIK / Shutterstock
220 © Anna Frajtova / Shutterstock
232 © tsaplia / Shutterstock
241 © Oldesign / Shutterstock
250 © ozzichka / Shutterstock
250, 251 © An Vin / Shutterstock
250, 251, 253 © Polina Tomtosova / Shutterstock
251 © memej / Shutterstock
252 © Anastasiya Zaplatina / Shutterstock
252 © SketchStudio / Shutterstock
252 © Nataliia Pokrovska / Shutterstock
253 © tsaplia / Shutterstock
253 © hchjjl / Shutterstock
253 © Margo Kukhar / Shutterstock
259, 260 © Drekhann / Shutterstock

About the Authors

Andy Min and Thomas Sullivan are the best friends and creative partners behind We Love You, a project dedicated to spreading hope and empathy in the disconnected online world. They have grown a devoted community of millions across Instagram, TikTok, and YouTube by creating playful, thought-provoking videos centered on a deep connection with the natural world. Whether they are in the lush Santa Cruz Mountains or the bustling city, they try their best to see good in the world and to share it with everyone they can. They also feel a little bit weird writing about themselves in the third person. They hope you like this book. They both live in Los Angeles, California.